PICTORIAL HISTORY OF
WORLD WAR II

PICTORIAL HISTORY OF
WORLD WAR II
Charles Herridge

Hamlyn
London · New York · Sydney · Toronto

Published by
The Hamlyn Publishing Group Limited 1975
London · New York · Sydney · Toronto
Astronaut House, Hounslow Road, Feltham, Middlesex, England

© Copyright The Hamlyn Publishing Group Limited 1975

ISBN 0 600 37104 2

Printed in Great Britain by Jarrold and Sons Limited, Norwich

ACKNOWLEDGMENTS

The publishers are grateful to the following for the illustrations reproduced
in this book:

Associated Press; Bavaria Verlag; Canadian Army; Central Press Photos;
Co-press; Christopher Ellis; Fox Photos; Hamlyn Group Library;
Imperial War Museum; Keystone Press Agency; Kyodo Photo Service;
New York Times; Novosti Press Agency; Paul Popper; Pictorial Press;
Radio Times Hulton Picture Library; SCR Photo Library; Snark International;
Staatsbibliothek, Berlin; Syndication International; Topix; Ullstein;
United Press International; US Navy; US Signal Corps; Roger Viollet;
Zeitgeschichtliches Bildarchiv.

Contents

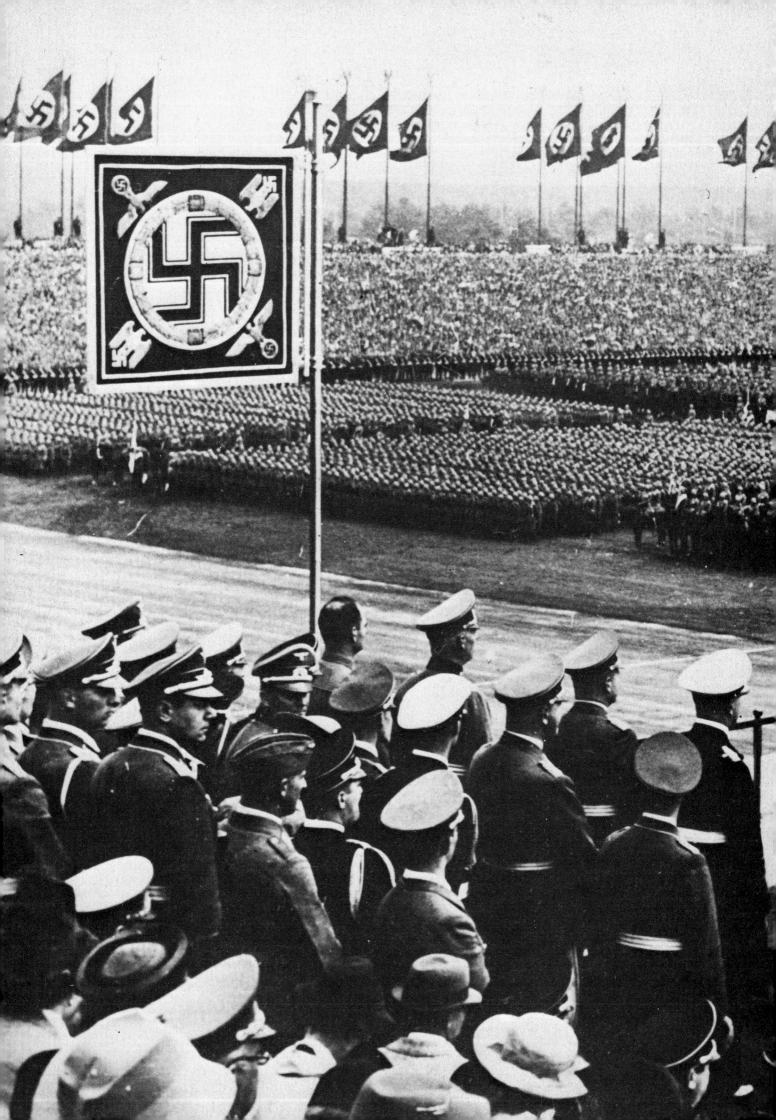

The Prelude to War

The signing of the peace treaties at the end of the First World War saw Germany humiliated and stripped of her possessions. She lost her territories overseas, and in Europe lost Alsace-Lorraine and East Prussia. Allied armies occupied the Rhineland, the size of her army and navy were stringently limited, and she was required to pay reparations for the First World War which soon brought about the collapse of her currency and produced massive unemployment.

It was thus in a Germany festering with discontent that Adolf Hitler first raised his voice. By appealing to the German people's conviction that they had been brutally oppressed by the victors of the First World War, he soon captured a large audience. He spoke of national greatness and Nordic racial superiority, he denounced Jews and Communists as those who had stabbed Germany in the back and brought about her defeat, and by an intensive programme of propaganda created a National Socialist Party which by 1932 had 230 seats in the German parliament and around thirteen million supporters. After President

◄◄
Nuremberg Rally, 1938. Hitler addresses assembled troops against the awe-inspiring backcloth created by his personal architect Albert Speer.

◄
American infantry parade through Trier at the end of the First World War, signalling the occupation of Germany by the victorious powers.

▼
A French armoured car rattles through the streets of occupied Essen in 1918.

▶
A German officer reduced to begging in the street after the First World War. This picture symbolises the depressed spirit of postwar Germany.

▶▶
Unemployed Germans in postwar Berlin. Hitler's early speeches capitalised on the destitution and broken pride of his countrymen.

The French occupation of the Ruhr in 1923 created, not surprisingly, enormous ill-feeling among Germans. Here a French soldier threatens an elderly civilian.

A smiling Hitler doffs his hat to appreciative supporters as he emerges from an early Nazi Party meeting in a Munich beer cellar in 1925.

14

A striking, though somewhat posed, view of Hitler with admirers in a beer garden. Throughout his career he was deeply aware of the importance of presenting a good image to the camera.

A one hundred billion mark banknote issued in response to the catastrophic inflation that overtook Germany in 1923. The Allies' punitive claims for reparation payments helped to create this situation.

Ernst Röhm (centre), head of the SA, with Group Leaders. Röhm organised the SA, the first Nazi private army, in 1921, and it soon became a formidable instrument of political terror.

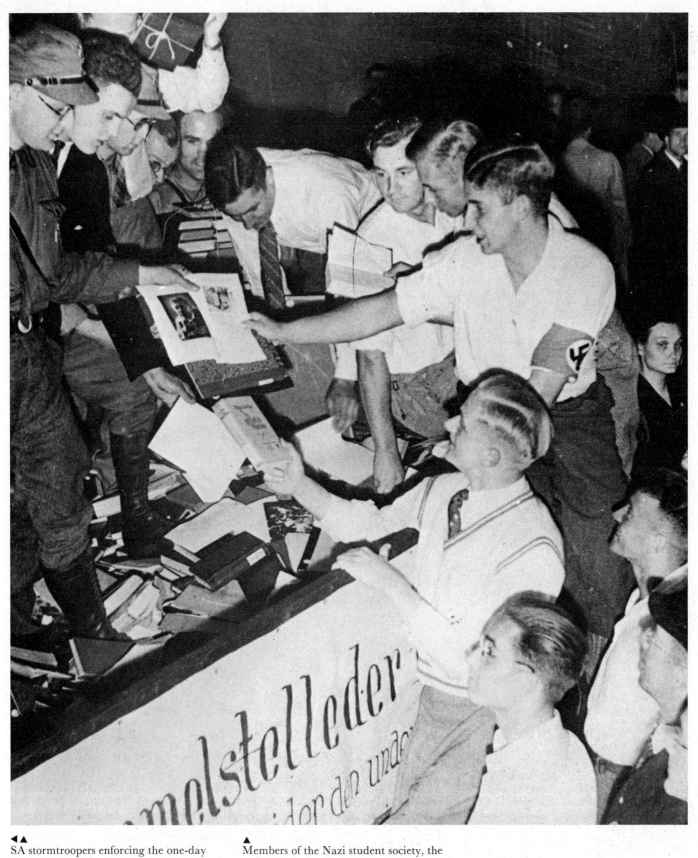

◀▲

SA stormtroopers enforcing the one-day boycott of Jewish-owned business on April 1, 1933. This kind of anti-Semitism was the forerunner of an unparalleled programme of atrocities.

◀

President Hindenburg, with Reich Chancellor Hitler on his right and Hermann Goering on his left, attends the memorial parade for the Battle of Tannenberg. Hitler was shortly to seize absolute power.

▲

Members of the Nazi student society, the Studentschaft, eagerly seize a consignment of 'un-German' books from a university library. In ten days in May 1933, no less than 500 tons of books were burned in Berlin alone.

Hindenburg's death in 1934, Hitler's power became absolute. In the summer of 1934 he ruthlessly purged his rivals and, having set aside the rule of law, established a totalitarian state.

He now embarked on a major programme of rearmament, in contravention to the Versailles Treaty but unhindered by its other signatories, and early in 1936 was confident enough to send German troops to reoccupy the Rhineland. Once again, the Allies made no attempt to stop him, and the operation was successful. Later in the year he and his Italian Fascist ally, Benito Mussolini, both sent help to Franco in the Spanish Civil War and signed a pact joining them in the Berlin-Rome Axis.

Hitler's primary preoccupation during this period was with Germany's

◄
From left to right, Nazi leaders Rudolf Hess, Hermann Goering, Julius Streicher and propaganda chief Josef Goebbels, perhaps the man most instrumental in rousing public support for Hitler.

◄▼
Abyssinians conducting the hopeless fight against Mussolini's invading Italians in 1935.

▲
Mussolini leads Italian *Bersaglieri* in their characteristic trotting march. His armies failed to live up to expectations in the forthcoming war.

▶
Members of the International Brigade, made up of volunteers from all over Europe, who fought on the Republican side in the Spanish Civil War. This war gave Hitler and Mussolini an ideal opportunity to test their new weapons.

need for *Lebensraum*, or living space. If she was to develop from a second-class nation into a major world power she must have room to expand, and if she was to support a rapidly growing population demanding prosperity she must have land for growing food, and raw materials for power and manufacturing.

He started by looking towards Austria, which already had a strong Nazi movement, but whose Chancellor was anxious to retain Austria's independence. Hitler's armies marched in nevertheless, and in 1938 entered Vienna unopposed. Hitler had succeeded by a combination of strong-arm diplomacy and skilful deployment of his propaganda machine.

Czechoslovakia was to be the next victim. The frontier region, known as the Sudetenland, had a German population which felt it was being unfairly discriminated against by both Czechs and Slovaks. The country was rich in natural resources, had a large army, and sported the big Skoda armament works. By stirring up the latent discontent of the German population Hitler was able to foment trouble in Czechoslovakia leading to an armed border confrontation. At this point the British prime minister, Neville Chamberlain, representing Czechoslovakia's supporters, Britain, France and Russia, went to Germany to try to appease Hitler. The outcome of a series of meetings was that unless the Sudetenland was joined to Germany, Hitler

German cavalry move into the Rhineland in March 1936. Hitler's reoccupation of this demilitarised area was a calculated risk, which he freely admitted later.

The occupation of the Rhineland: a German artillery regiment receives the acclaim of the people of Freiburg.

In March 1938 Hitler annexed Austria. Here Swastika-waving Austrians welcome German troops in Salzburg.

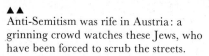

▲▲
Anti-Semitism was rife in Austria: a grinning crowd watches these Jews, who have been forced to scrub the streets.

▲
German troops enter Prague. Hitler broke his promise to occupy only the Sudetenland border country, and annexed the whole of Czechoslovakia.

▶
Hitler receives the salute of Austrian Nazis as he parades through Vienna. The existence of a strong Nazi movement in Austria played a large part in Hitler's scheme for the annexation.

◀

Winston Churchill, whose warnings in the British Parliament of Hitler's true intentions went largely unheeded, climbs out of an RAF aircraft of 615 Squadron.

▲

On the left, Neville Chamberlain who fruitlessly pursued a policy of appeasement of Hitler until it was too late. He is shown here with Mussolini, Lord Halifax and Count Ciano at the Rome Opera House.

▶

The move which finally provoked an armed reaction from Britain and her allies: the invasion of Poland. German infantrymen smash a frontier barrier to make way for their armoured columns.

would start a war, but that if his territorial claims in Czechoslovakia were granted, he would make no further territorial claims in the rest of Europe. France and Britain agreed — in spite of their promises of protection to Czechoslovakia — and Hitler, breaking in turn his promise, later moved into the whole of Czechoslovakia. He judged that Britain would not be prepared to fight for Czechoslovakia, and that France would not want to fight alone — and he was right — but next time, when he invaded Poland, they declared war.

As history was later to prove, the declaration came much too late. The vacillations of the Western powers had allowed Hitler to achieve an armed strength and a position in Europe which were to take six years of bloodshed to dislodge.

The Struggle Begins

A German soldier surveys the destruction left in the wake of the Wehrmacht's advance in Poland.

German Foreign Minister von Ribbentrop and Joseph Stalin beaming after the signing of the Nazi-Soviet Pact in Moscow in 1939.

Hitler's demands on Poland began by being, in the circumstances, almost modest: all he required, he said, was the return of the German port of Danzig and free access to it and East Prussia through Poland, the 'Polish Corridor'. Poland was not inclined to accede to this request, and, seeing that Britain had reacted violently to his occupation of Czechoslovakia, Hitler did not press his case too strongly at first. After all, Britain had redoubled her armaments drive and had given Poland an unqualified guarantee of her protection. But he realised that the guarantee was worthless without Russian support from the East, and, anticipating that the British would jump to seek this support, set about bringing Russia around to his own side. The Russians had been brushed off by the British when earlier they had offered an alliance, and were not unwilling, after overcoming their initial mistrust, to make an agreement with Hitler, particularly as this promised a chance of regaining pre-1914 Polish territory.

London. Sunday, September 3, 1939.
A newspaper-seller tells it all.

German troops mopping up Polish
resistance in the battered streets of Warsaw.

▶
Polish soldiers in one of the fortified
positions in the suburbs of Warsaw
surrender to the Germans.

▼
Hitler watches as his victorious troops
parade, goosestepping, through the streets
of Warsaw.

Russian infantry marches into Poland from the east as Hitler's forces close in from the west. Once conquered, Poland was divided between Russia and Germany.

◄

After the invasion of Poland there followed a period of uneasy quiet, the Phoney War. It was at this time that London's children were evacuated to the countryside.

Blitzkrieg Tactics

1 Initial Concentration

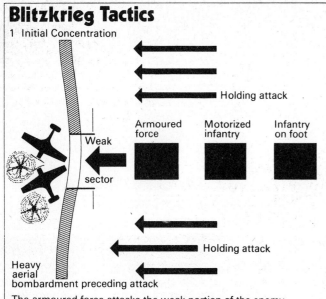

Holding attack

Armoured force

Motorized infantry

Infantry on foot

Weak sector

Holding attack

Heavy aerial bombardment preceding attack

The armoured force attacks the weak portion of the enemy position where gaps, weak anti-mechanized defence, favourable terrain etc favour operations of mechanized forces. It is supported by intensive air attacks and artillery concentrations. Motorized divisions follow close behind the armoured units, and are in turn followed closely by infantry divisions on foot.

Blitzkrieg Tactics

2 Breakthrough

Holding attacks

Armoured units

Motorized infantry

Armoured units

Motorized infantry

Infantry on foot

Armoured units

Motorized infantry

Armoured units

Holding attacks

The breakthrough is achieved. Armoured and motorized units widen the gap and advance to seize the objective, supported by aviation and artillery. Infantry on foot follow close behind to relieve the armoured and motorized units.

▶ German troops being ferried ashore in Oslo harbour during the invasion of Norway in April 1940. The invading forces arrived on land, by sea and from the air. In the background lies a German pocket battleship.

▶▲ Wrecked shipping at Narvik after an attack by British warships in April 1940. Only in her naval operations in the Norwegian theatre could Britain claim any degree of success.

▶▼ British prisoners being marched off by their German captors after the failure of Britain's countermeasures in Norway.

Once this, the Molotov-Ribbentrop pact, was signed, Hitler's way was clear, and on September 1, 1939, German forces crossed the Polish frontier. There followed the first demonstration of the effectiveness of mobile warfare combining armoured and air forces. The Poles concentrated their armies well forward, near the long frontier, and their reserves were thinly spread. Thus, when Hitler's armoured columns, supported by the Luftwaffe, pierced the Polish defences, the Polish troops, marching on foot, were unable to draw back fast enough to regroup. In a neat pincer movement Bock and von Rundstedt, from north and south respectively, thrust their army groups towards Warsaw. On September 17 Russian troops crossed the eastern frontier, and despite gallant resistance Warsaw fell on September 28.

In the West, the British and French had achieved little, partly because of slowness in mobilisation, partly because of outdated tactical ideas. In the East, Poland fell because her army, relying still on massed cavalry charges, was an anachronism, thrown into confusion by the merciless onrush of Hitler's compact and highly mobile forces.

Germany and Russia divided Poland between them, and Russia went on to make considerable territorial demands from Finland, which the Finns resisted. A war followed in which the Finns fought hard and bitterly, but by March 1940 the issue was decided.

The collapse of Poland was followed by what became known as the Phoney War, which lasted till the spring of 1940. During these months

◄▲
On April 9, 1940, German forces crossed the Danish frontier. One hour later they invaded Norway. Here a German column waits at a roadside in Denmark, while an anti-aircraft gun stands by to repel attackers.

◄
German transports in a Copenhagen square after Denmark's capitulation.

▲
Finnish hussars advancing towards the front during the war between Finland and Russia, which on the Finnish side was fought with great gallantry against overwhelming odds.

the Allied leaders considered one offensive plan after another – and reached no conclusion – while Hitler, an October peace offer having been rejected by the Allies, developed his plans for an early and decisive offensive against France. The sooner he launched his offensive, the less prepared the French would be to meet it, and once France had fallen, he was certain Britain would negotiate for peace. However, time, his generals and the weather were against him, and even when he had at last fixed January 17 as the start of the offensive, an extraordinary incident put paid to his plans. A German officer flying from Münster to Bonn lost his way and landed in Belgium. He was arrested and was found by his captors to have with him Germany's complete operational plan

for the attack in the West, forcing Hitler to call off the offensive. When the new plan, the Manstein Plan, was put into effect, it held a few disastrous surprises for the Allies.

In the meantime, and to his adversaries' consternation, Hitler struck north, suddenly, at Norway and Denmark. On April 9, 1940, German forces landed at a number of points along the coast of Norway, and also entered Denmark. By the end of the day they had taken Oslo and the major ports of Trondheim, Bergen and Narvik, while Denmark lasted only twenty-four hours. How did these two countries fit into Hitler's scheme? Most of Germany's iron ore for her war production effort came from North Sweden via Narvik – and Hitler wanted to safeguard the sea passage from Norway, fearing

The face of this Russian prisoner in Finland bears the marks of strain and fatigue. The Finns did not give up as easily as the Russians had expected.

A unit of Polish cavalry. In 1939 the Polish army still fielded eleven horsed cavalry brigades, at least one of which charged German panzers during the invasion.

A German Stuka dive-bomber. A vital factor in Blitzkrieg warfare, its vulnerability to modern fighter types was later exposed in the Battle of Britain.

that Britain would occupy Norway while Denmark offered a valuable food supply.

When Hitler struck, Britain came to Norway's aid, landing troops near Narvik and Trondheim. But they were too late, for the Germans had by then established a strong enough position to be able to beat off their attackers, helped by overwhelming air superiority. For the British, the sink-ing of a flotilla of German destroyers in two actions in Narvik fjord, one involving the battleship *Warspite*, was but small consolation for the complete failure of the Norwegian campaign. For Hitler, it meant security of iron-ore supplies and a base for aerial attacks on Britain, and, later, on Russia-bound convoys. Once again, German forces had moved too fast for their opponents.

The Battle of France

◄◄
The invasion of Belgium was launched at the same time as the invasion of Holland. Advancing German soldiers sprint past blazing wreckage across a road.

As the Allies' campaign in Norway drew to a close, Hitler launched his offensive on the West, which was to culminate in the evacuation of the British Expeditionary Force from Dunkirk and the fall of France.

It started with successful assaults on Holland and Belgium. Landings of airborne troops at The Hague and Rotterdam were timed to coincide with attacks on Holland's eastern frontier, and this combination proved highly effective in creating the confusion the Germans needed. German armoured forces broke through a gap in the south and sped across the country to join up with the airborne forces at Rotterdam, while the Luftwaffe kept up a relentless pressure from the air. Five days after the initial

assault the Dutch capitulated.

Belgium was the next to feel the effects of Hitler's Blitzkrieg treatment. Here again the German attack came from the land and from the air. Two major objectives had to be secured before the main invasion could be launched: the capture, intact, of two key bridges across the Albert Canal, and the silencing of the Belgians' powerful fort at Eben Emael. A ground attack would move slowly enough to allow the Belgians to blow up the bridges and to make the best possible use of the guns of Eben Emael — so small detachments of airborne troops were dropped silently out of the sky. The bridges were secured, the fort was silenced, and German troops moved across the

▶
On May 10, 1940, German parachute troops were dropped behind the Dutch lines. This was the first major airborne attack of the war, and took the Dutch by surprise.

▶▲
German paratroops move into action after landing in Holland.

▶▼
An artillery unit of the Dutch army.

41

canal, penetrating the Belgian line of defence on the other side. Two panzer divisions raced through the gap thus created and soon the Belgian forces were in general retreat. British and French forces were moving up to support them when, following Manstein's brilliant plan, von Rundstedt's army group, after pushing through the Ardennes, emerged on the banks of the Meuse. This surprise move caught the Allies off their guard. They had not imagined that the Germans would attempt to launch a major offensive through the wooded hills of the Ardennes, difficult country for tanks and motor vehicles. By launching a major offensive against the onrushing Germans in the north, and maintaining a strong defensive concentration on the Maginot line in the south, they had left a poorly defended gap at the uncompleted western end of the Maginot line — which is exactly where the Germans turned up. Led by the bold tank commander, General 'Fast Heinz' Guderian, panzer infantry and tanks, with Luftwaffe air support, were soon across the Meuse. Once on the other side, their rapid advance would have continued unchecked but for the German High Command's sudden failure of nerve. Fearing an Allied counterstroke, it halted Guderian's progress until the infantry had had a chance to catch up with him, then gave him the green light. His panzer corps swept onwards towards France's northern coastline.

This movement, the British were not slow to realise, would trap their forces between the Germans advancing through Belgium from the east, Rundstedt's army group to the south, Guderian's panzer corps in the west, and the English Channel to their north. Soon Guderian had reached

▲
German infantry filing across a makeshift bridge at Maastricht, Holland. The retreating Dutch had blown up the bridge.
◄
The city of Rotterdam during a German bombing raid. It was almost completely razed to the ground by the Luftwaffe.
►▲
British and French troops were poured in to stem the tide of the German advance through Belgium. This picture shows a British machine-gun post at a street corner in Louvain.
►
While fierce fighting raged in Belgium, German panzer forces were nosing through the Ardennes, to emerge on the banks of the Meuse, here being crossed.

The Maginot line: the underground railway passing the stores. This enormously expensive military white elephant was the ultimate rationalisation of First World War tactics – the complete surrender of initiative to the enemy.

General Guderian's panzers spearheaded the German thrust through France from the Ardennes. He is here seen with radio operators in his command vehicle.

◀
A photograph taken by General Rommel
of a shell explosion just ahead of his car
during the push through France.

▲▲
German soldiers using a flamethrower
against one of the bunkers on the Maginot
line. Manstein's plan for the western
offensive involved bypassing the strongest
points on the line.

▲
Rommel flies over a halted column of
German tanks in a valley in northern
France, on a reconnaissance flight.

the north coast, cutting the BEF off from Boulogne and Calais. It now became clear that the British troops would have to be evacuated by sea, and when the Belgian army surrendered, the race was on. The only port of embarkation left open was Dunkirk, and even that was threatened by the panzer corps that lay a mere ten miles to the west.

Had Hitler chosen to order it, the BEF could have been annihilated or forced to capitulate at this point, but for motives which have never been clearly identified, he held off, and the now-legendary evacuation of Dunkirk began. Harassed by constant Luftwaffe attacks, the armada of ships and boats that sailed from Britain to take part in the evacuation brought back a total of 338,000 Allied troops.

Hitler's reluctance to finish off the BEF while it lay within his power may have had many causes, among them, perhaps, an expectation that the British would want to make peace with him. However, it did have the single, telling effect of leaving 338,000 Allied troops ready to fight against him another day. The British were thus able to ward off the subsequent threat of invasion, and ultimately this contributed to Germany's defeat.

Yet the Battle of France was not over. The French forces had been severely depleted, while the Germans had brought up reinforcements and replacements. Without so much as a pause for breath the Germans launched a new offensive against the French front along the Somme

◄
Viscount Gort, commander-in-chief of the British Expeditionary Force that was evacuated from Dunkirk, with the French General Gamelin, commander-in-chief of Allied Forces during the Battle of France, who was replaced by Weygand before the Dunkirk evacuation.

◄▼
A trawler, heavily laden with troops, heads out to sea from Dunkirk.

►
British infantry wading out from the beach at Dunkirk to a waiting rescue vessel.

▼
British and French troops docking on their arrival in Britain. 338,000 Allied troops reached safety.

Battle of France

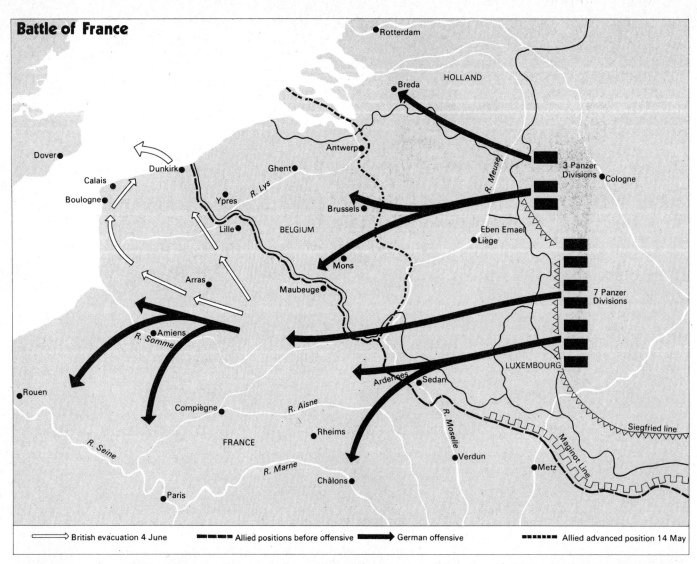

Dover ● • Dunkirk • Calais • Boulogne • Ypres • Lille • Arras

R. Lys — Ghent ● • Antwerp • Brussels • Mons • Maubeuge

Rotterdam ● • Breda ● HOLLAND

BELGIUM

R. Meuse • Eben Emael • Liège

3 Panzer Divisions • Cologne

7 Panzer Divisions

LUXEMBOURG

Amiens • R. Somme

Rouen ● • Compiègne • R. Aisne • Rheims • R. Moselle • Verdun • Metz

R. Seine • FRANCE • R. Marne • Châlons ● • Paris

Ardennes • Sedan • Siegfried line • Maginot Line

| ⇨ British evacuation 4 June | ▬ ▬ ▬ Allied positions before offensive | ➤ German offensive | ▪▪▪▪▪ Allied advanced position 14 May |

Rommel receives the surrender of a French corps commander and a British divisional commander at St Valery on June 12, 1940.

A motorcycle combination pulls over as tanks rumble past in Hitler's Aisne offensive, which, following hard on the heels of Dunkirk, was the beginning of the end of the Battle of France.

German troops assemble in the Place Vendôme after the fall of Paris on June 14, 1940.

German artillery pounds the Maginot line.

► Hitler in a jubilant mood just before the signing of the French armistice on June 22, 1940, in the same railway carriage that witnessed the armistice at the end of the First World War.

▼ A Pzkw Mk II ploughing through heavy country in the Ardennes. For all their vaunted armoured spearheads, it is often overlooked that the German army relied on horse-drawn transport for as much as 75 per cent of their infantry divisions.

and the Aisne. Initial resistance was fierce, but after two days the line was pierced by Hoth's panzer corps near Rouen and the defence collapsed. On June 14, 1940, only ten days after the last boatload of soldiers had left Dunkirk, and only nine days after the new offensive began, German troops entered Paris. The French Government had left for Tours on June 9, German forces were driving deep into France, fragmenting the French army into small groups, and the situation appeared hopeless. On June 25 Marshal Pétain signed an armistice with Hitler in the same railway coach that had witnessed the signing by Germany of the 1918 armistice.

Events so far, culminating in the sudden collapse of resistance in France, had conclusively proved the effectiveness of Blitzkrieg warfare. With comparatively small mobile forces, and with only light and medium tanks, Hitler had, in an extremely short space of time, taken possession of or brought under his control most of Western Europe. Every time he moved, he moved too fast for his opponents – in Norway, Denmark, Holland and Belgium – while the brilliant execution brought France and Britain to their knees at a speed which even Hitler had not expected. For Britain, left now as she was to fight alone, the prospects were bleak.

The Battle of Britain

RAF Hurricanes in formation above the cloud layer climb to engage raiders reported heading for London.

An aerial photograph of part of Hitler's Operation Sealion invasion fleet lying in Boulogne harbour. It was in order to soften up British resistance that Hitler ordered Goering to launch an aerial assault on Britain.

The fall of France and the evacuation of Dunkirk would have left Britain, her army in disarray and her air force not yet up to adequate strength, open to devastating assault by Germany, had it been launched immediately. But Hitler held back, firstly because arrangements and preparations for the seaborne invasion of Britain, known as Operation Sealion, were far from complete, and secondly because he hoped that Churchill, reviewing Britain's perilously weak situation, would seek peace negotiations with Germany. The terms of such a peace, Hitler felt, would be highly favourable to both parties: Britain would withdraw from the conflict and allow Hitler to continue unmolested towards domination of Europe; and Germany in her turn would undertake to leave Britain and her overseas empire alone.

Churchill, however, made no moves to enter such negotiations, and, with Sealion postponed to September, Goering was instructed to launch a major air assault on Britain to soften up possible resistance to the invasion when it came. Hitler's navy and army chiefs heaved a sigh of relief. They had always been sceptical of the chances of the invasion's success, as it would be an operation of stupendous logistical and tactical complexity, and were

▲
British Home Guard volunteers practise firing at aircraft.

◄
Positions of friendly and hostile aircraft being plotted on the operations table at a Royal Observer Corps centre. All new developments would be instantly passed on to Fighter Command.

▼
The British had the advantage of possessing radar equipment during the Battle of Britain. The picture shows the outline of a German bomber on a radar screen.

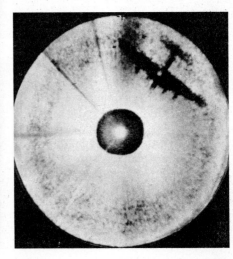

therefore lively in their encouragement of Goering's desire to please the Führer by demonstrating the supremacy of the Luftwaffe's airpower.

On August 5 Goering received the order to go ahead, and the Battle of Britain began. Goering had at his disposal some 2,700 aircraft – a considerably greater number than the British could muster. Nevertheless, both sides possessed nearly equal numbers of fighters, and Britain had three points in her favour. She had a radar network backed up by spotters from the Observer Corps; she was able to build planes faster (to replace losses); and her Spitfires and Hurricanes, having less far to fly to the combat area, had fuel to stay in combat longer. On the debit side, the Hurricane was slower than the German Me 109 (though the Spitfire was slightly faster), and the RAF was short of trained pilots, a fact which emerged as the battle wore on.

The Germans called August 13 *Adlertag*, or Eagle Day. It signalled the launching of an armada of 1,400 German planes, with orders to destroy RAF bases and radar installations south-east of London. However, the

first moves did not live up to Goering's expectations. The British radar and spotter network enabled the RAF to have its aircraft in the air ready to meet the Luftwaffe, and for a loss of forty-five German planes Goering could only report serious damage to two British bases and the destruction of thirteen RAF planes. Cloudy weather restricted the Luftwaffe's activities on the following day, August 14, but on August 15 came the biggest onslaught of the whole battle. Over 1,500 German aircraft, more than a third of them bombers, crossed Britain's coasts. This was Goering's attempt to crush his opponents' aerial resistance with one blow. There were two attacks on airfields in the north of England: fierce resistance forced one bomber force, escorted by Me 110s which failed to provide much protection, to turn back without causing serious damage; the other, though unescorted, inflicted heavy damage on the RAF base at Duffield in Yorkshire in spite of heavy losses.

In the south of England, Hawkinge and Lympne were attacked, Lympne being temporarily put out of action. Throughout the day, in a bewildering

▲
Goering and his Air Staff officers watch the fighting over Britain from the north coast of France. Goering himself directed operations.

▶▲
A Spitfire aircraft being rearmed for combat. The Spitfire was faster than the German Messerschmitt Me 109, and Spitfire pilots, having less far to go to the combat zone than their opponents, had the additional advantage of having fuel to stay in combat longer.

▶
Pilots await the order to scramble.

ILY MIRROR, Monday, Sept. 16, 1940.

Daily Mirror

SEPT 16

No 11,473   ONE PENNY
Registered at the G.P.O. as a Newspaper.

175 MASS RAIDERS DOWN

A HUNDRED AND SEVENTY-FIVE GERMAN RAIDERS WERE DESTROYED UP TO 10 p.m. YESTERDAY. FOUR FELL TO THE A.A.

The R.A.F. had one of its greatest days in smashing two mass attacks on London.

Thirty of our machines were lost, but ten pilots are safe.

The two raids came in little over two hours.

In the first Buckingham Palace was again bombed. The King and Queen were not there.

Crowds in London streets cheered and danced with joy as they saw a bomber crash.

Pictured on right is a Dornier crashing in flames.

Yesterday's German losses bring up to over 2,000 the total of enemy planes destroyed since the beginning of the war.

BOMB HIT QUEEN'S APARTMENT

THE Queen's private apartments were badly damaged when Buckingham Palace was bombed again yesterday—for the third time in a week.

But the King and Queen escaped the murderous attack. They were not in the palace when the bombs fell. There were no casualties.

The raider was shot down soon afterwards. It was engaged by British fighters and shot to bits.

Two high explosive bombs and a shower of incendiaries were dropped. Neither of the high explosive bombs has yet exploded. The first fell in the Queen's apartments and the second on the lawns.

The incendiary bombs scattered over the Palace grounds, where they started several small fires on the grass.

These fires were quickly dealt with by the Palace A.R.P. staff and police.

Break in Pieces

Watchers said that they saw the German plane high over the Palace and heard the whistle of bombs.

"Then we saw British fighters attacking the plane," said one. "A few seconds later we saw the plane break in pieces and the wings go fluttering in one direction while the fuselage fell almost like a stone.

"One of the crew jumped, but his parachute failed to open and he fell on the roof of buildings close by. He was killed instantly."

In the first attack on the Palace a delayed action bomb was dropped last Monday. It exploded on Tuesday, damaging the Princesses' swimming pool.

On Friday a raider swooped down and released a salvo of five high explosive bombs. One of these wrecked the Royal Chapel.

After Friday's raid the King declared in reply to the Cabinet's congratulations: "Like so many other people the Queen and I have now had a personal experience of German barbarity which only strengthens the resolution of all of us to fight through to final victory."

Every One a Hero

Mr. Anthony Eden, Secretary of State for War, has sent a message to bomb disposal units praising their courage and devotion to duty.

"Your cheerful acceptance at all hours of hazards which might well daunt the stoutest heart is beyond praise," he says. "Your work has aroused the admiration of your fellow countrymen and is worthy of the high traditions of the Army."

ST. PAUL'S SAFE —TON BOMB IS RACED AWAY

ST. PAUL'S CATHEDRAL has been saved from the biggest bomb ever dropped on London. The bomb weighed a ton.

For three days soldiers risked their lives to dig it clear. Two lorries were needed to haul it out.

Then it was loaded on to a fast lorry. All the way from St. Paul's to Hackney Marshes the route was cleared of traffic, and the lorry with its deadly load was driven through at high speed to be safely exploded. In charge of the bomb disposal section on this highly dangerous job was Lieutenant R. Davies.

The bomb had been dropped in Dean's Yard, close to the west end of St. Paul's. It fractured a six-inch gas main and three of the soldiers were gassed at an early stage.

Officer Drove

When the gas had been cut off the bomb disposal section had to dig 27ft. 6in. into the subsoil before they found the bomb.

It looked like a vast hog, about 8ft. long. It was fitted with fuses which made it deadly dangerous to touch or move.

To save devastating damage to St. Paul's, the risk of removal had to be undertaken.

Two lorries in tandem were used to haul it out of the hole, and Lieutenant Davies himself drove the lorry which took the bomb to the marshes, the risk of explosion being imminent all the time.

At Hackney Marshes yesterday the bomb was blown up by the bomb disposal section. It caused a 100ft. crater. It rattled windows and loosened plaster in houses far away on the marshes.

Only the courage and tenacity of the officer, his N.C.Os and men prevented . . . velled to the ground.

The closed roads around St. Paul's were yesterday reopened for traffic.

Hunted Down by R.A.F.

THE R.A.F. gave the German Air Force its most gruelling day ever yesterday—and its most costly day for nearly a month.

Four hudnred enemy machines were launched in two mass raids.

Most of those that escaped were chivvied and harried to the coast.

Spitfire and Hurricane squadrons, many of them veterans in London defence, fought the raiders over the Kent coast as they came in, fought them over Maidstone and Canterbury, above the Medway and Thames Estuary.

Many they turned away. The survivors they fought again over London itself.

Squadron after squadron of fighters flew into action.

A squadron of Hurricanes, which destroyed nine, began their fight over London and ended up over the cliffs of Hastings. Another chased a group of bombers from the Thames at Hammersmith to Beachy Head, shooting down five.

A formation of Hurricanes which caught some of the enemy just as they were coming up the Thames handled them so roughly that one of the pilots said afterwards he thought it was very unlikely that any of the bombers

Continued on Back Page

The end of a raider over London at noon yesterday. High up you see a Dornier plunging to destruction—tail and wing-tips already shot away. n the bottom corner the British fighter that did it is seen. Between the two is a German parachuting down. Other pictures on centre pages.

◄◄
The RAF's biggest bag of successes: the *Daily Mirror* jubilantly announces the figure.

▲
German airmen being marched away from the blazing wreckage of their He 111 aircraft on Britain's south-east coast.

◄
Group Captain A.G. 'Sailor' Malan, one of Britain's top-scoring fighter aces, clambers into the cockpit. With thirty-five victories, he was the RAF's third highest scorer.

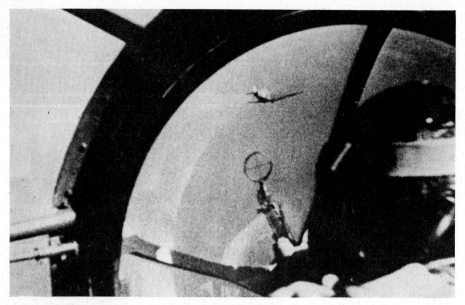

◀ ▲
A Spitfire seen from the nose of a Heinkel He 111 as it dives through a German bomber formation.

▲
Major Adolf Galland (left), a leading German air ace. He was the German top-scorer in the Battle of Britain, with fifty-seven victories.

◀
A German fighter, trailing smoke and flame, begins its final earthward plunge.

◀▼
The German Messerschmitt Me 109 was more difficult to manœuvre than the Spitfire and, although possessing considerable combat advantages, was hampered by a range of only 400 miles.

▶▲
An Me 110 over England during the Battle of Britain. Although the Luftwaffe had high hopes for this type, it proved too clumsy and vulnerable to be effective.

▶
A formation of Heinkel He 111 bombers thunders through a cloudy sky on its way to London. After the British raid on Berlin, Hitler ordered Goering to concentrate on bombing London.

variety of raids, the Germans had the British fighters chasing around after them. Fortunately for the British, the German raids were not well co-ordinated and could therefore be fended off, but when two massed raids on the south of England were launched in quick succession in the evening, the British were forced to mount a massive response. To meet the first raid, as many as 170 fighters took to the air – a tribute to the co-ordination and control of Fighter Command. Both raids were beaten off, having inflicted little damage.

The Luftwaffe's losses that day totalled seventy-six aircraft, compared with British losses of thirty-four. It was becoming apparent to the Luftwaffe that mastery of the air over Britain was a harder objective to achieve than expected, but on August 16 and 18 further large-scale bombing raids were launched. Both raids achieved little, and German losses were severe. Goering had overestimated English losses, and, believing that the RAF was so weakened in numbers that the use of radar was no longer a crucial factor, he had concentrated his efforts on RAF bases rather than radar installations. But he was wrong on both counts, and paid for his mistake with the loss of over 450 aircraft in the first three weeks of August.

On August 24, after a brief lull, Goering launched his second

▲
Roof-spotters on duty during an air raid over London. Their task was to direct fire-fighters to where they were needed.

▲▲
A Heinkel He 111 bomber flying over London's Silvertown. By switching the attack to London, Hitler surrendered all chance of winning the Battle of Britain.

offensive against a beleaguered Britain. The RAF's superiority up till this time had not been achieved without cost: there had been heavy aircraft losses, which were not being matched by the rate of production of new aircraft; factories and airfields had suffered considerable damage; pilots were overstretched and ex-hausted; and new pilots were not coming out of the training colleges fast enough to replace those lost. Moreover, Goering's tactics improved, and the latter part of August saw a frightening increase in British losses. But the Luftwaffe's losses had con-siderably reduced its power, and when on September 7 Hitler instructed Goering to switch from his policy of incessantly pounding RAF Fighter

A pall of smoke rises from burning buildings beside the Thames. London's dockland was an important target for bombers.

▶ ▶
The morning after: fire-fighters work on, exhausted, in a wrecked street in Coventry.

Command to a series of daylight bombing raids on London, Fighter Command was given a chance to regain some of its strength. On that day Goering and Kesselring stood on the cliffs of France's northern coast and watched a massive armada of 1,000 German aircraft drone over their heads towards London. The docks and central and east London were bombed, 1,600 civilians being killed or injured. Anti-aircraft and fighter opposition were both weak — there were insufficient guns and the RAF arrived on the scene late — and a further German force sent over the same evening lost only one aircraft in night-long attacks.

There followed the series of nightly attacks on London, lasting until

▲
While the bombs drop overhead, Londoners do their best to settle down for the night in an Underground station. They slept here night after night.

◄
A building blazes during the Blitz. From September 7 to November 13, 1940, the Luftwaffe dropped more than 13,000 tons of high explosive on London, killing one person for each ton that fell. Nearly a million incendiaries also rained down on the capital.

◄ ▼
Like browsers in a bookstore, these gentlemen inspect the rare volumes in the burnt-out library of Holland House, near Kensington High Street, London. The house, built in 1607, was severely damaged by incendiaries.

► ▲
In a street in East Ham, East London, people salvage what they can from their bombed houses. This scene became all too familiar as the Blitz wore on.

►
The man who inspired the British to keep on fighting, Winston Churchill, here seen being cheered by crowds in Liverpool, which also was a target for German bombs.

November 3, known as the 'Blitz'. Despite their shaky start, the British were soon giving the Luftwaffe an even rougher ride. Anti-aircraft defences were considerably stepped up and Fighter Command, benefiting from the respite afforded by the relaxation of pressure on its bases, soon gained in strength.

By September 14, target date for the launching of Operation Sealion, the invasion fleet was ready, but Goering had destroyed neither the RAF nor London, and the invasion was postponed. It could not be postponed for long, however, before weather conditions turned against it, and on the morning of September 15 Goering and Kesselring ordered 1,000 aircraft over London in a massive daylight raid. In a battle which raged all day, sixty German aircraft were shot down, RAF losses being twenty-six, and finally, British defences remaining unbroken, the attack was repulsed.

On September 18 the order was given for the Sealion fleet, with bad weather threatening and under persistent attack from RAF bombers, to be dispersed. The whole purpose of the German aerial assault on Britain — the softening-up for the invasion — had failed, and although bombing went on for some time, the climax had passed.

On November 3, for the first time in months, no air-raid siren warned Londoners of an impending attack. However, a new offensive was on the way. On November 14 a campaign of night bombing raids began on cities, industrial centres and ports. Coventry was the first to suffer, then Birmingham, Southampton, Bristol, Plymouth and Liverpool. London was the target of a heavy attack on December 29, then the Luftwaffe eased off for the winter. In March the raids started again, and on May 10 London suffered a very violent assault, but on May 16 the Luftwaffe shifted its attention to the impending invasion of Russia and the worst was over.

In this famous battle Germany came a great deal closer to victory than Britain admitted or Hitler thought. Had British bombers not bombed Berlin on August 25, Hitler would not have ordered the Luftwaffe to concentrate on bombing London, and the attack on Fighter Command's forward bases could have been pressed home at a time when the RAF was at its weakest. And if later the Luftwaffe had persisted longer in its attacks on industrial centres, Britain would have been brought to her knees. Two tactical errors, analogous to his mistake in not finishing off the BEF at Dunkirk, loosened Hitler's stranglehold on Britain — and she survived to fight another day.

The Invasion of Russia

German panzers carrying infantry during the rapid advance into Russia in October 1941.

Hitler's pact with Russia, the Molotov-Ribbentrop pact of 1939, was a strategic expedient which had enabled him to invade Poland and subsequently overrun the West without fear of intervention from Russia. But, bearing in mind his fanatical anti-Communist convictions, it is hardly surprising that he should later invade the territories of his erstwhile ally. His motives, however, were not purely ideological. In the long term Russia offered almost un-

limited *Lebensraum*, the wheatfields and granaries of the Ukraine, and oil from the Caucasus. In the short term he felt she wàs threatening his oil supplies from Rumania, and was conspiring to intervene on the British side in Germany's war against Britain. Britain, he insisted, must be conquered – therefore Russia must be knocked out.

Towards the end of 1940 General von Paulus, who later was to command the army that surrendered to

In the half-light of a misty dawn, a German machine-gunner guards a river crossing in the advance into Russia.

German troops snatch a few moments' relaxation in the summer sunshine as they are ferried on pontoons across a river in Russia. This picture is illustrative of the confident German mood in the early stages of the Russian campaign.

The moment of firing. German field artillery on the Russian front.

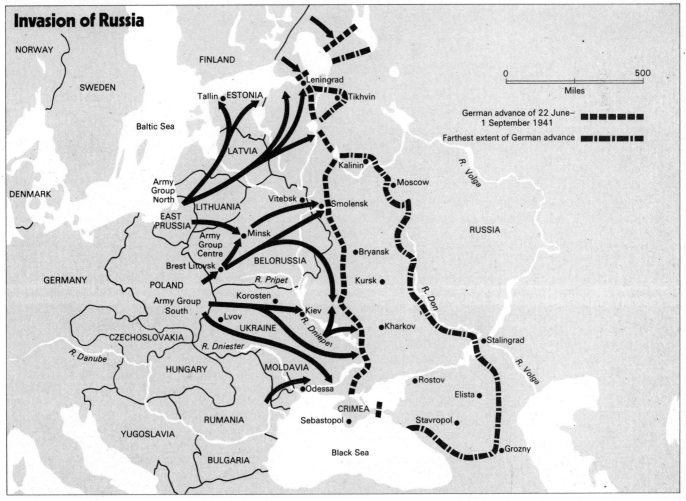

Invasion of Russia

NORWAY

SWEDEN

FINLAND

Baltic Sea

DENMARK

GERMANY

Tallin • ESTONIA

LATVIA

LITHUANIA

EAST
PRUSSIA

Army
Group
North

Army
Group
Centre

Brest Litovsk

POLAND

Army Group
South

Lvov

CZECHOSLOVAKIA

R. Danube

HUNGARY

YUGOSLAVIA

RUMANIA

BULGARIA

Leningrad

Tikhvin

Kalinin

Moscow

Vitebsk • Smolensk

Minsk

BELORUSSIA

R. Pripet

Korosten

Kiev

UKRAINE

R. Dniepel

R. Dniester

MOLDAVIA

Odessa

CRIMEA

Sebastopol

Black Sea

Bryansk

Kursk

Kharkov

R. Don

R. Volga

RUSSIA

Rostov

Elista

Stavropol

Stalingrad

R. Volga

Grozny

0   500
                Miles

German advance of 22 June–
1 September 1941

Farthest extent of German advance

▲
German infantry fan out as they advance across a ripening field.

▶
A Russian prisoner in the Ukraine, his face lined with apprehension as he faces the camera of his Nazi captors.

the Russians at Stalingrad, was instructed by Hitler to make a detailed plan for the offensive against Russia. On December 5 Hitler issued orders for preparations to be made for Barbarossa – the invasion of Russia – which were to be complete by May 15, 1941. Indeed, the invasion would probably have taken place on that date had Hitler's attention not been diverted by the despatch of German troops to the Balkans.

Hitler had wanted to secure control of the Balkans by armed diplomacy before invading Russia, thus forestalling any British intervention in this quarter. Bulgaria knuckled under, but Greece and Yugoslavia resisted, compelling Hitler to divert panzer divisions intended for the Russian offensive to overrun Greece and Yugoslavia. Britain's armed intervention was almost completely ineffectual, and in a matter of weeks

▲
A German soldier lashes out with the butt of his rifle at the legs of a Russian prisoner in the Ukraine.

◄
General Karl von Rundstedt, who commanded the German advance on Kiev.

◄▲▲
The Russian veteran Marshal Budenny, whose army faced von Rundstedt when he advanced on Kiev. In the subsequent battle 600,000 Russians were cut off in a pincer movement by Kleist and Guderian, whom Hitler had diverted from their advance on Moscow to help von Rundstedt smash Budenny's army.

◄▲
German infantrymen heaving a gun carriage on to a raft while a Russian village blazes behind them.

◄◄
A mocked-up German official propaganda photograph, showing Hitler rubbing his hands with glee as he surveys a landscape littered with dead Russian soldiers.

▲
Russian villagers mourn their dead. The advancing Germans slew thousands of Russian civilians.

Greece and Yugoslavia were brought to heel. But the start of Barbarossa had to be postponed till the second half of June, and this was later to contribute to the German defeat in the East.

Early on June 22 German troops flooded across the Russian frontier in three separate thrusts. In the north, an army group under von Leeb advanced on Leningrad through the Baltic States occupied by Russia; in

the centre, an army group under von Bock moved from the Warsaw area towards Smolensk and then Moscow; and in the south von Rundstedt led an army group south of the Pripet marshes towards Kiev.

Hitler intended that these armies should drive as far into Russian territory as possible, then wheel inwards and trap the Russian defenders in a series of massive envelopments. Initially the advance went

77

▶ As the Germans pressed nearer, Russian women were organised to dig deep anti-tank trenches round Moscow.

▼ Red Army tanks, with supporting infantry, advance on German positions round Moscow.

almost as speedily as it had done in Poland and France, but the Germans had reckoned without the stubbornness of the Russian resistance, which held them up longer than they expected. Additionally, the roads were poor and the distances to be covered, far greater than those involved in the Polish or French campaigns, created considerable logistical problems. Hitler's frustration mounted as his forces plunged deeper and deeper into Russia and the grand encirclement still eluded them. Then it started to rain. The unsurfaced roads turned to mud and the advance gradually became bogged down. Tanks and other tracked vehicles could continue unimpeded, but their supplies and supporting infantry, in

◄
German infantrymen spring back amid shellfire as the Russians push them back. The German advance was abruptly halted at Moscow.

▼
A German half-track pauses during the advance. In the background commandeered Russian cars are being rounded up.

79

Battle of Kiev

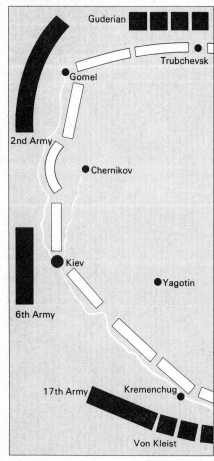

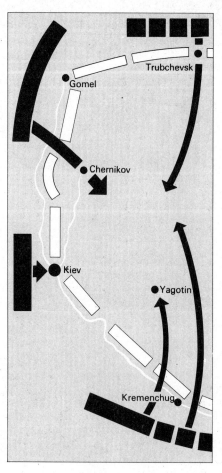

Guderian

Trubchevsk

Gomel

2nd Army

Chernikov

Kiev

Yagotin

6th Army

Kremenchug

17th Army

Von Kleist

☐ Budenny's Army Group   ■ German Armies   ■■■ German armoured Groups

▶▲
German infantry, following the path of destruction laid by Stuka dive-bombers, race towards blazing buildings abandoned by the Russians.

▶
German infantry wait tensely in the undergrowth during the final push towards Kiev.

▼
A German panzer column strikes towards the heart of Russia.

wheeled vehicles, slowed them down.

In spite of these problems, the panzer groups of Guderian and Hoth were able to capture 300,000 Russian troops at Smolensk in July, and had it not been for the slow progress of von Rundstedt's armies in the south, the advance towards Moscow would have proceeded apace. But Rundstedt found himself opposed at Kiev by a formidable Russian army under the veteran Marshal Budenny. Hitler was anxious that Rundstedt should be enabled to push on with maximum speed to the Crimea, and, in the face of Guderian's insistence that he should keep the Russians on the run down the highway towards Moscow, Hitler ordered part of Bock's army group, including Guderian's panzer corps, to turn south and help Rundstedt defeat Budenny and his Russians at Kiev. Guderian, thrusting south, and Kleist, thrusting north,

met east of Kiev in a brilliant pincer movement which encircled some 600,000 Russians, but it was the end of September before the advance got under way again. Another encirclement by Bock's armies round Vyasma yielded a further 600,000 prisoners, but the weather was worsening and fresh Russian forces were assembling before Moscow.

The German generals thought the time had come to halt for the winter and consolidate their position — even Hitler had lost some of his optimism — but Bock was for going on, and at the beginning of December German troops reached the suburbs of Moscow, only to be summarily bundled out by the Russians under Zhukov. Hitler ordered his forces not to retreat but to establish positions as near to Moscow as possible, and there they stayed throughout the appalling Russian winter, ill-clothed and ill-equipped for the conditions.

In the south, Rundstedt's armies had moved into the Crimea and the Donetz basin, but had failed to take the oilfields of the Caucasus, and by the first week of December they were in retreat. Hitler's failure to take Moscow can be attributed to the tactical error of diverting the armies headed for Moscow to help out Rundstedt at Kiev; to his underestimate of the size of the Russian armies that faced him, which always seemed to have fresh troops to bring forward when losses were suffered; and to the mud that slowed down the advance from June onwards.

The next year was to witness the beginning of Nazi Germany's downfall enacted in Russia — at Stalingrad.

◀
Hitler would not countenance a withdrawal from Moscow at the end of 1941, and his troops, ill-equipped to survive the savage conditions of a Russian winter, were ordered to hang on. They wrapped themselves up in anything they could find.

▲
German prisoners are paraded through Moscow by their Russian captors. The diversionary move to defeat Budenny's army at Kiev had held up the advance on Moscow long enough to allow the Russians to assemble a large army to defend the city.

▶
Russian troops dug in round Moscow in the winter of 1941–42 keep watch for any movement on the German side.

America Before Pearl Harbor

Throughout the 1930s America maintained a policy of strict isolation where events in Europe were concerned. When Mussolini attacked Ethiopia in 1935, Congress passed an Act preventing the President, Roosevelt, from intervening on either side. Similarly, when the Spanish Civil War broke out, Congress insisted on America adopting a neutral stance, prohibiting arms shipments to either side. Tied down by such legislation, Roosevelt could do no more, as the situation in Europe grew more and more menacing, than exhort Americans to adopt a more outward-looking attitude, in the hope that public opinion would gradually turn against the Fascist régimes in Europe that posed a threat, however distant, to world peace. But even the occupation of Czechoslovakia, the invasion of Poland, and the declaration of war by Britain and her European allies, failed to engender a unified move towards the abandonment of America's neutrality.

When France fell, however, and only Britain stood between Germany's aggression and the United States, popular feeling changed overnight. At last Congress gave the go-ahead to a programme of mobilisation and to measures providing for the supply of aid to Britain. First, surplus arms were sent; next, a deal exchanging fifty US First World War destroyers for British naval bases was concluded; and finally Congress passed a Lend-Lease Bill providing for the supply of war equipment to the opponents of Fascism on easy payment terms. By the time Roosevelt had finished his talks with Churchill aboard the battleship *Prince of Wales* off Newfoundland in August

Gas-masked Japanese troops make a run for it in a Shanghai street in 1937.

▶
President Franklin D. Roosevelt broadcasting to the nation.
▼
Winston Churchill with British Minister for Supply, Lord Beaverbrook, aboard HMS *Prince of Wales* prior to their meeting with Roosevelt off Newfoundland in 1941.
▶▶
From a hilltop position Japanese soldiers keep watch in China.

The destroyer *Shaw* was hit by three bombs, which exploded her forward magazine. Her severed bow lies on its side in the foreground.

A small boat rescues a seaman from the crippled battleship *West Virginia*. Beyond her lies the *Tennessee*.

Japanese Zero fighters were used in the Pearl Harbor attack. They had a maximum speed of 330 mph, and were light and highly manœuvrable.

Japanese soldiers pay obeisance to their emperor before the rising sun. This scene is illustrative of their fanatical patriotism. To the Japanese, the emperor was immortal.

1941, it was clear that America's neutral stance was so in name alone, for she had committed herself to the Allied side.

Hitler did not fail to appreciate this. He became even less favourably inclined towards the United States when she took steps to safeguard the arrival of supplies shipped across the Atlantic by offering convoy cover. German U-boats first attacked American ships in May 1941, and when American shipping in the security zone off the eastern seaboard became a target for U-boats towards the end of the year, the United States made its final preparations for action, though no declaration of war was issued. It was during this uneasy period that Japan attacked Pearl Harbor.

America and Japan had been at loggerheads for some time, the principal issue being Japan's attempts to bring China, by warlike means, under her domination. The Sino-Japanese War had begun in 1937, provoking American protests, the United States having a strong interest in China. Japan's refusal to heed these protests prompted the US Government to declare an embargo on the export of certain materials to Japan, including petroleum, which gradually tightened its grip. Deprived of a major source of fuel, the Japanese had two alternatives: to accept a humiliating agreement with America's terms regarding the inviolability of China; or to look elsewhere for petroleum

sources – if necessary by force.

Failing to secure an agreement with the Government of the Dutch East Indies for petroleum supplies, the Japanese decided to negotiate once more with the United States in the summer of 1941, hoping there was still a chance of breaking the embargo on acceptable terms. If this failed, they would have to resort to force in the Indies. It did fail, as each side's attitude hardened.

Towards the end of 1941 it seemed that war was inevitable, and both sides hastened preparations for it. To gain time, a Japanese envoy was sent to Washington in the middle of November. He was to present Japan's last offer, the rejection of which was a foregone conclusion, but was to keep the discussions going until Japan was ready to attack. The Americans also played for time. Finally, as Roosevelt learned of Japan's intention to sever diplomatic relations, Japanese aircraft struck at the American naval base at Pearl Harbor, on the Hawaiian island of Oahu.

This happened at 8 am on December 7, 1941. The American fleet and airfields were sitting ducks, and within only half an hour the damage was done. Seven battleships were destroyed or badly damaged. Only the aircraft carriers escaped, being absent at the time. Having maimed the US Fleet, the Japanese could now proceed with their programme of conquest in the Pacific.

Japan Overruns the East

◄◄
Japanese troops occupy Rangoon during their headlong advance in Burma in May 1942.

▼
Japanese troops crouch on an invasion barge as they prepare to land on Luzon in December 1941. This was the first stage in their conquest of the Philippines.

▼▼
Native Philippine troops surrender to the Japanese on the Bataan peninsula.

The successful attack by the Japanese on the American naval base at Pearl Harbor on December 8, 1941, effectively removed, as the Japanese had intended it to do, the threat of American intervention in their operations in the South West Pacific. A number of other operations, simultaneous with the Pearl Harbor attack, were to lead to the extraordinarily rapid collapse of Western resistance in the Far East.

The first to fall was Hong Kong, which had the inherent weakness of

being only 400 miles from Japanese air bases on Formosa while at the same time being 1,600 miles from the British base at Singapore. Hong Kong was attacked from the mainland on December 8 by a strong Japanese force which, after initial repulses, landed in the north-east corner of the island and thrust southwards, splitting the defending forces in half. Eighteen days after the operation began, Hong Kong's garrison surrendered.

Again on the same day as the

The 'march of death' on Bataan. US prisoners of war after the Japanese invasion.

The British battle-cruiser *Repulse*, which on December 10, 1941, was sunk by Japanese bombs and torpedoes off Malaya, along with the battleship *Prince of Wales*. This was a severe blow to Allied seapower in the East.

Crewmen from the sinking *Prince of Wales* transferring to a destroyer alongside. Eight torpedoes from Japanese bombers sent her to the bottom.

A column of Japanese tanks advancing through Malaya finds its way barred by deliberately felled trees.
▶
Oriental resourcefulness: the Japanese fitted railway wheels to enable road vehicles to speed up their supply systems in Malaya.

attack on Pearl Harbor, Japanese aircraft struck at American air bases on the largest Philippine island, Luzon. Their attack caught the Americans off their guard, and a sizeable proportion of the American aircraft on Luzon were damaged or destroyed, giving the Japanese the air superiority that was to work so much in their favour in the conquest of the Philippines. The US commander on Luzon was General Douglas MacArthur, who disposed of about 110,000 Philippine troops and some 30,000 regulars. The former, inadequately trained, were deployed round the long coastline of the island, while the regulars were concentrated close to Manila. When the first Japanese troops, commanded by General Homma, landed on Luzon, they had little difficulty in breaking through the defences of the Philippine army and were soon thrusting inland towards Manila. At this point MacArthur withdrew his forces into the fortified Bataan peninsula, this movement being successfully completed by January 6, 1941, in spite of Japanese attacks on the retreating Americans. The area occupied by MacArthur's troops behind their defences on the peninsula amounted to a mere fifty miles of malaria-ridden country. The Americans, cut off from reinforcements, resisted bravely for two months, their numbers decimated by fever. The Japanese, too, were cut down by malaria, but received fresh troops in March and gradually pushed the defenders down towards the tip of the peninsula. On April 9 the American commander (in MacArthur's absence) surrendered.

A Japanese onslaught now descended on the island of Corregidor, a mere two miles from Bataan, whose garrison sustained a terrible pounding from Japanese aircraft and from artillery sited on

▼
Japanese soldiers form a living bridge as their comrades cross a stream in the humid Malayan forests.
▼▼
Japanese transports drive across a causeway in the rear of the advance.

Bataan. By early June it was all over and the remaining forces surrendered, leaving the Japanese masters of the north Philippines.

The fourth Japanese operation, begun on December 8, 1941, involved landings at three points on the Malay peninsula, at Singora, Patani and Kota Bharu. Their aim was to take Malaya and wrest the vital naval base at Singapore, which symbolised the whole of Western armed presence in the East, from British hands. All these landings were made on the east coast, but while a diversionary force advanced down the east of the peninsula, the main force moved across and entered Malaya on the west side.

At this point British seapower in the East was dealt a heavy blow which was greatly to facilitate the Japanese conquest of Malaya and Singapore. The modern King George V Class battleship *Prince of Wales*, in company with the older battle-cruiser *Repulse*, was steaming under the command of Admiral Phillips to intercept Japanese transports which had just made a landing at Kuantan on the Malay peninsula, when the two ships were attacked by a large force of Japanese bombers and torpedo-bombers. Lacking cover from an accompanying aircraft carrier (there being none available at the time) the ships could only defend themselves with anti-aircraft fire, and within two and a half hours both ships, struck repeatedly by accurate Japanese bombing, had sunk. Their destruction allowed the Japanese

programme of landings to go forward unchecked and hastened the end of Malaya and Singapore. Meeting ill-organised resistance, and backed up by unquestionable superiority in the air, the invading Japanese, under General Yamashita, conquered Malaya in under two months. On January 31, 1942, the remnants of the British forces in Malaya crossed the straits to Singapore Island.

The defence of the island was hampered by the fact that its naval base had been constructed to resist attack from the sea. Thus when the Japanese came through the back door, landing on the island in force on February 8, they were quickly able to establish a foothold. Though outnumbered by the defenders, the Japanese were better led, better trained and better supported from the air. They were soon driving the British southwards, and in spite (or

◄
Japanese light tanks in Singapore.
◄ ▼
Civil defence fire-fighters turn a hose on the smouldering ruins of bombed houses in Singapore.
►
General Percival, British commander at Singapore, on his way to surrender. The Japanese took 60,000 prisoners.
▼
British soldiers in Singapore eye their Japanese captors warily. Though fewer in numbers, the Japanese were better organised than the defenders of the island city.

because) of Churchill's exhortations to fight to the death for the honour of the Empire, the British forces, numbering around 60,000 in all, surrendered after a week, on February 15, with Singapore blazing around them. This was one of the worst setbacks ever suffered in British military history.

The fall of Singapore was to be followed closely by the Japanese entry into Rangoon on March 8 and the subsequent British retreat over the Indo-Burmese border into India. The conquest of Burma saw the fulfilment of Japan's strategic objectives in the Eastern theatre: the establishment of an insurmountable defensive barrier from the Philippines to the Indian frontier behind which they could pursue uninterrupted their desired aim of bringing China under Japanese control. Additionally, they could ensure the oil supplies from which the American embargo had cut them off.

The conquest of Burma was achieved by a comparatively small Japanese force. It began in the middle of December 1941, with an advance northwards into Burma from Malaya and Thailand. The defending British forces were soon on the retreat, and by early March, when the Japanese were close to Rangoon, the western gateway to China, their commander, General Sir Harold Alexander, decided not to attempt to hold the city. The aim was to fall back on and defend Mandalay, which would still give the British a link with China via the Burma road. But the Japanese pressed on, receiving heavy reinforcements of troops and planes, and soon it became clear that Mandalay could not be held either.

The British now began a 200-mile withdrawal towards the Indian border, and by early May were safely across it. Casualties far exceeded those of the Japanese, though the majority were saved, but Burma, Thailand, Malaya and Singapore were now firmly in Japanese hands. The defensive barrier was complete – within six months of Pearl Harbor – and Britain had lost her entire footing in the East.

◄▼ Japanese infantry crawl into a blazing town during their rapid conquest of Burma.

▶ Light tanks of a Japanese mechanised unit cross an emergency bridge in Burma, built to replace the one destroyed by the retreating British.

▼ The stricken British cruiser *Cornwall* settles in the water on April 5, 1942. Along with her sister ship, *Dorsetshire*, she was intercepted and sunk by Japanese torpedo-bombers in the Indian Ocean while steaming to meet Admiral Somerville's fleet in the Maldive Islands.

The Desert War 1940-43

A member of an 8th Army patrol crawls forward under shellfire during First Alamein.

At the point when the battle for France could be seen to have swung decisively in Hitler's favour, Italy came into the war, led by Benito Mussolini. He saw that France would soon collapse and that Britain would therefore be left in a lonely and exposed position — an ideal moment, he thought, to unseat Britain from her position in the Mediterranean and Africa and to add to Italy's overseas possessions.

At that time a small British army in Egypt, under General Sir Archibald Wavell, faced an Italian force in Cyrenaica, under Marshal Graziani,

which was vastly superior in numbers. Before Graziani had had time to mount an offensive, Wavell moved out of Egypt in a lightning stroke which was to yield sweeping results in a very short space of time — the kind of action, in fact, that was to characterise the see-sawing fortunes of both sides in the desert war. Moving over the Egyptian frontier, British raiding forces, including the 7th Armoured Division which was to earn the 'Desert Rats' nickname, took Fort Capuzzo from the Italians on June 14, 1940. Graziani countered this threat by advancing eastwards

General Archibald Wavell, commander of British forces in Egypt in 1940 on the outbreak of the desert war.

Matilda tanks churn across the desert. In the hands of the 7th Royal Tank Regiment they did sterling work in North Africa.

North African Theatre of War

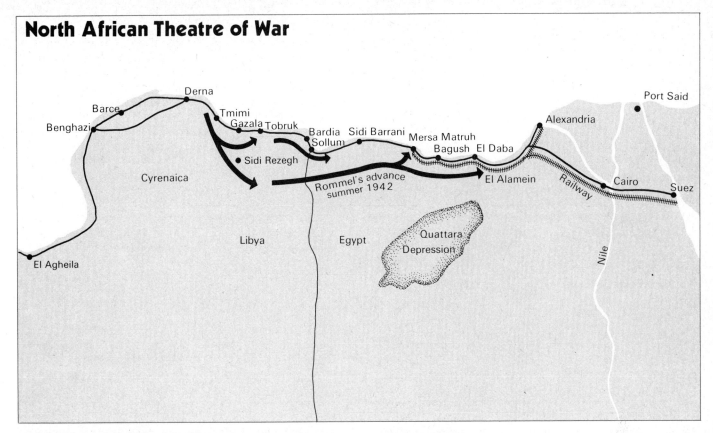

◀

A column of Italian troops captured in December 1940 during the British advance westwards. The Italians surrendered in vast numbers.

on September 13 and establishing a chain of camps round Sidi Barrani, which Wavell ordered General O'Connor to attack. On December 7 British raids on the camps began, spearheaded by the Matilda tanks of the 7th Royal Tank Regiment, and in three days the Italians were in flight, 40,000 of them being taken prisoner. This resounding success was followed by the capture of the Italian-held coastal fortress of Bardia, where 45,000 Italians were taken prisoner, and, later, a westward drive culminat-

ing in the capture of the key port of Tobruk on January 21, 1941, together with a further 30,000 prisoners. Throughout the campaign, the Matilda tanks had played a critical role.

By now O'Connor was desperately in need of reinforcements and new equipment, but Churchill's mind was fixed on sending troops to help the Balkan countries resist Italy and Germany, and reinforcements were withheld. However, O'Connor was given permission to press on westwards

General Erwin Rommel, who arrived in Libya in February 1941 to try to restore the situation. The 'Desert Fox' is here seen talking to German officers.

◀▼
A German mobile column raises dust in Rommel's counter-offensive early in 1941. By mid-April he had pushed the British back into Egypt.

▶
A German tank drives across the desert.

▼
Australian infantry defend the perimeter of Tobruk with a captured Italian 7 5-mm gun.

with the aim of taking the port of Benghazi. As the advance proceeded, reconnaissance revealed that the Italians were getting ready to leave Benghazi for El Agheila, taking the coastal route, and in spite of his depleted resources O'Connor boldly decided to try to cut them off by racing across the interior and intercepting them as they rounded the headland. The Desert Rats pushed across the desert and took up positions at Beda Fomm, and on February 6 the retreating Italians were routed, 20,000 being taken prisoner.

With the Italian forces now in disarray, prospects for finally pushing them out of North Africa by advancing into Tripoli were excellent, but Churchill, still convinced of the greater importance of the Balkan theatre, called a halt. The next development, a fateful one for the British, was the arrival of General Erwin Rommel, later to become known as the 'Desert Fox', to bolster up the Italian forces in Libya. He arrived on February 12, and his presence proved so decisive that by mid-April the entire British force, with

the exception of the garrison bottled up in Tobruk, had been pushed back over the Egyptian border. Seeing that the British advance had halted, he decided, though with quite inadequate forces at his disposal, to take the offensive. He quickly recaptured the El Agheila bottleneck and swept on to Benghazi, which he took. On April 14 he laid siege to Tobruk, which was gallantly defended by the 9th Australian Division under General Leslie Morshead, but he failed to pierce the defences and by the first week in May the siege had been called off.

He now planned to press forward into Egypt, but was denied reinforcements because Hitler was giving priority to the invasion of Russia. The result was that Germany now lost a perfect opportunity to gain a decisive victory and expel Britain from North Africa.

There was to be little time, however, for a change of mind, as Wavell now received the help he had so long been waiting for. His Balkan ambitions shattered, Churchill sent a convoy to North Africa through the

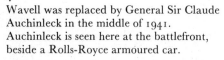

▼
Wavell was replaced by General Sir Claude Auchinleck in the middle of 1941. Auchinleck is seen here at the battlefront, beside a Rolls-Royce armoured car.

8th Army Cruiser tanks re-form near Sidi Rezegh after their clash with the Afrika Korps panzers. This tank battle resulted in victory for Rommel.

South African troops, one holding a hand-grenade, search ruined houses in Sollum in January 1942.

Long Range Desert Group patrols meet in the desert.

Scots Guards move forward, protected by Matilda tanks and under cover of a smoke and dust screen, during First Alamein.

perilous Mediterranean, bearing a large consignment of new tanks. When they arrived, a British counter-attack was mounted. On May 13 Wavell launched Operation Brevity, designed to join up with and relieve the beleaguered Tobruk garrison. It failed, and by the end of May the British were back inside Egypt once again. Next, in mid-June, came Operation Battleaxe, a major attempt to regain the initiative, but in the course of it the British lost ninety-one tanks to the Germans' twelve, and it too failed to make an impression.

Churchill now was all the more determined to win the desert campaign, and poured in men and equipment. Wavell was replaced by General Sir Claude Auchinleck, and plans were prepared for the next offensive, Operation Crusader, which was launched in mid-November. It involved a double movement: one force was to hold down Rommel's frontier forces; the other was to sweep round his flank, destroy his armour, and push on to Tobruk. In its attempts to pin down Rommel's highly mobile armour, the flanking force became dispersed, but eventually Sidi Rezegh, twelve miles south-west of the Tobruk defence perimeter, was reached. Here a major tank battle took place that resulted in victory for Rommel's forces, though at a cost of seventy precious tanks. While the British were recovering from this blow, Rommel struck suddenly at their rear, aiming to cut off their communications. He moved swiftly towards the Egyptian frontier, but the attack lost momentum through poor communications and shortage of fuel, and eventually he turned back. The

▼
General Bernard Montgomery, victor of the Second Battle of El Alamein who arrived to replace Auchinleck in August 1942.

Battle of Gazala

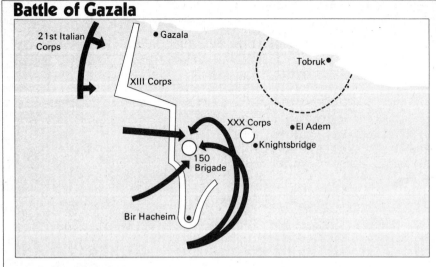

21st Italian Corps

Gazala

Tobruk

XIII Corps

XXX Corps

El Adem

Knightsbridge

150 Brigade

Bir Hacheim

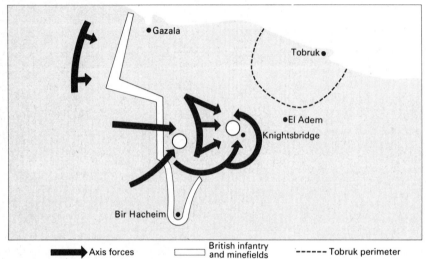

Gazala

Tobruk

El Adem

Knightsbridge

Bir Hacheim

▶ Axis forces   ▢ British infantry and minefields   ----- Tobruk perimeter

British now managed to break through to Tobruk, and Rommel withdrew to the El Agheila bottleneck, arriving in January 1942.

While there he received fresh tanks and equipment, and on January 21 he moved eastwards again, taking Benghazi and soon reaching the Gazala line, fifty miles west of Tobruk. After some fierce fighting, the British stronghold at Gazala fell, and Rommel moved on to Tobruk, which he took in June, together with 35,000 prisoners and a mass of valuable stores. This was a disaster for the British, ranking second only to the surrender of Singapore, and soon they were in full retreat back into Egypt with Rommel in hot pursuit. In this headlong eastward drive, he crossed the Egyptian frontier and pushed the British back to within sixty miles of Alexandria.

Here, at El Alamein, the British counterattacked. Rommel's troops were tired, their supplies low, and their tanks few in number, but the British attack was not strong enough to turn his advance into retreat. Nevertheless, the advantage went to the British, for although their losses were about the same as Rommel's, they could afford them and he could not – and the advance was indeed halted.

Early in August 1942 General

◄
The battle of Gazala, a classic envelopment, in which Rommel's Afrika Korps overran the southern flank of the British 8th Army holding the Gazala line.

◄▼
Tanks move into action on the first day of Second Alamein in October 1942.

▶
A Sherman tank being restocked with shells during Second Alamein. Shermans arrived in large numbers from America during the build-up to the battle, and contributed greatly to the superiority of the Allied armoured strength. Only Rommel's new Panzer IVs could match them, and of these he had a mere thirty.

▼
British infantrymen advancing towards enemy positions after Rommel's defeat at Second Alamein take cover behind a knocked-out German tank as a shell explodes close by.

118

Bernard Montgomery flew out to replace Auchinleck. He decided not to take any offensive action until he had had time to build up strength for a decisive victory, but on August 30 Rommel, now reinforced, struck at the British position on the Alam Halfa ridge. He was unable to make the progress he had planned, and eventually was forced to withdraw through shortage of fuel. Montgomery decided not to follow up with an attempted coup de grâce, preferring to continue his preparations for a later offensive, but the Alam Halfa battle, which had been well conducted and well fought, gave the British forces a great shot in the arm, while finally wresting away the initiative from Rommel.

By October 23 Montgomery was ready, and the Second Battle of El Alamein began. Rommel was ill and his forces were vastly outnumbered both on land and in the air. The battle opened with a massive combined barrage and bombardment of the Axis positions, but the first British thrust, Operation Charge, was blocked, and Montgomery put into action Operation Supercharge, a narrow-fronted attack launched against the weak Italian Trento Division in the centre, which took Rommel by surprise. On November 4 the Axis defences were breached and Rommel began to retreat. Though Montgomery gave chase, Rommel's forces escaped and were soon back at the El Agheila bottleneck.

The North African campaign now entered a new and final phase. The British victory at El Alamein had been a decisive one, and Rommel saw that from now on he could do no more than hold up the British advance for as long as possible. In addition to this pressure from the east, he now had to face a threat from the west, for British and American troops had landed in Morocco and Algeria on November 8 in the first stage of Operation Torch.

Throughout the Russian campaign Stalin had been urging Churchill and Roosevelt to open a second front

◀
As Rommel's forces retreat westwards through Libya, a Bofors gun passes a German lying dead beside the track.

◀▼
The speed of Rommel's withdrawal westwards strained the 8th Army's communications. Here a Hurricane fighter prepares to escort a Lockheed Hudson transport aircraft, loaded with supplies for forward units, from a captured airfield in Libya.

El Alamein

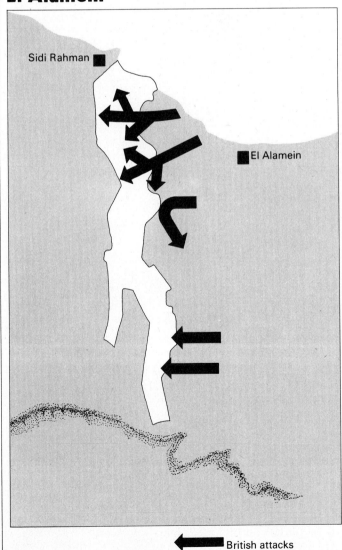

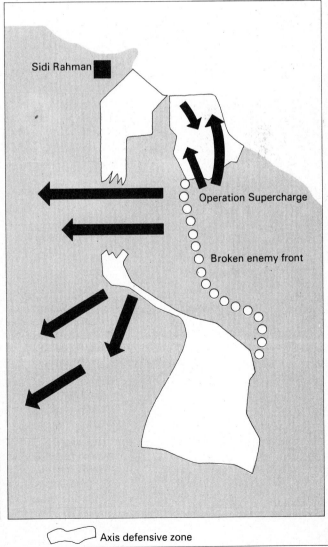

Sidi Rahman

El Alamein

Sidi Rahman

Operation Supercharge

Broken enemy front

◀━ British attacks

Axis defensive zone

▲
Three US generals – Roosevelt, Allen and Patton – observe action during the final stages of the Battle of Tunisia, after the Torch landings.

▶

An armoured car on night patrol during the drive to Tripoli fires at an enemy position.

and thus divert at least a part of German attention and effort from the Russian front. After some discussion, two possibilities had emerged: an invasion of Normandy, which Roosevelt favoured; and landings in North Africa, which Churchill opted for. The former was chosen, but when Rommel broke into Egypt in the middle of 1942, Churchill managed to persuade Roosevelt of the serious implications of Rommel's threat to the Suez Canal, and plans were laid for North African landings instead, under the codename Operation Torch.

The landings took place at Casablanca, Oran and Algiers. Resistance from Vichy French forces was either overcome or sidestepped, but this delayed the commencement of operations in Tunisia long enough for Axis troops there to make successful offensive moves and establish excellent defensive positions against Allied assaults from east and west. The Allies did not want to push into Tunisia until they had reached full strength, but when December came they saw that Axis forces had been considerably increased and this, together with the onset of bad weather, delayed the push into Tunisia until February 1943.

Rommel, whose forces were guarding the eastern approaches, realised that if the Germans did not take offensive action, Allied forces would soon have them hopelessly trapped from both sides, and he immediately advocated an offensive in the west, where the Allies were weaker. But

the German commander in the west, General von Arnim, made only a half-hearted attack, which failed to stop the Allied advance, and Rommel was forced to race westwards to his aid. He was beginning to make some headway against the Allies (having taken the Kasserine Pass) when he had to rush back eastwards to avert a mounting threat from Montgomery's forces. He arrived too late, however, and gradually the Axis armies were pushed back from both sides into northern Tunisia. Hitler refused to sanction a Dunkirk-style evacuation, and by May 12, 1943, all Axis forces had surrendered. The war in North Africa was at an end. Mussolini had failed utterly to make the territorial gains he had so coveted at the outset; Churchill, by pouring in reinforcements in 1941 to boost Operation Crusader, had done so at the expense of British strength in the Far East, thus indirectly contributing, perhaps, to the disastrous collapse of British resistance at Singapore; and Hitler, by sending huge reinforcements to his embattled armies in Tunisia, and failing to evacuate them before it was too late, left Sicily and Italy short of troops to repel the Allied landings, allowing the first stage of the Allied conquest of Europe.

▲
A British tank at full speed gets a near miss from an enemy bomb during the advance through Libya.

▶
The end of the North African campaign, May 1943. Thousands of German and Italian prisoners await transportation. Hitler's refusal to countenance an evacuation left him deprived of a large body of troops which he could have used to fend off the Allied invasion of Sicily and Italy.

The Battle of the Atlantic

◄◄
The scuttled wreck of *Graf Spee*, shattered by internal explosions, smoulders in the River Plate estuary in December 1939.

▼
A splendid picture of the British battleship *Royal Oak*, torpedoed and sunk in the naval base at Scapa Flow in 1939.

Hitler's strategic aim in the Battle of the Atlantic was to disrupt to the greatest possible extent Britain and her Allies' supplies of food and war materials. It was his U-boat arm, skilfully commanded by Admiral Dönitz, that claimed the greatest degree of success, but, happily for the British, Hitler and his navy chief Raeder persisted too long in their belief in the paramount importance of large surface ships, with the result that the U-boat force was never, till too late, developed sufficiently to gain an outright victory, though by March 1943 the Allies' position was extremely precarious.

The struggle lasted throughout the war, reaching a peak from mid-1942 to mid-1943. It began on

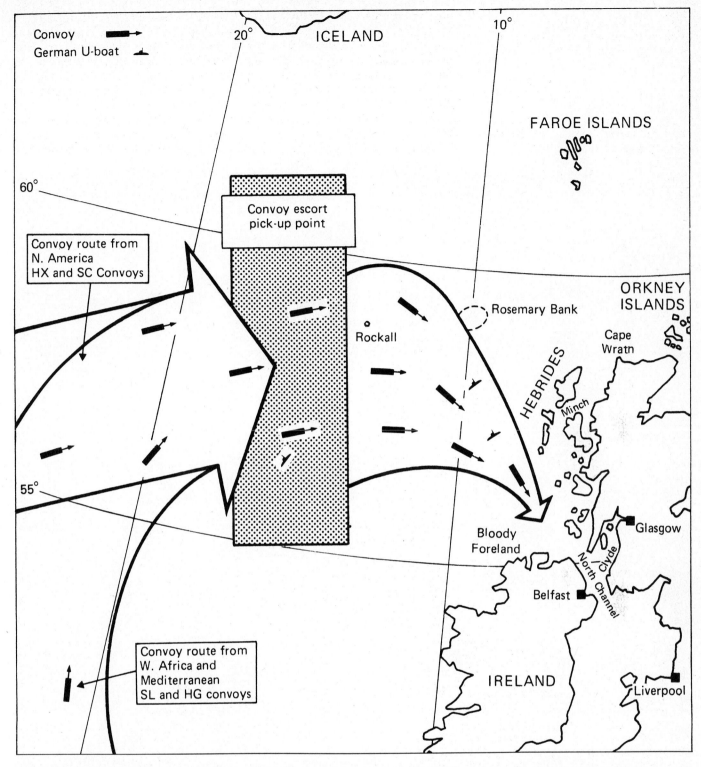

Convoy   ➤
German U-boat ⟂

Convoy escort
pick-up point

Convoy route from
N. America
HX and SC Convoys

Convoy route from
W. Africa and
Mediterranean
SL and HG convoys

20°   ICELAND

10°

FAROE ISLANDS

60°

55°

ORKNEY
ISLANDS

Rosemary Bank

Rockall

Cape
Wrath

HEBRIDES

Minch

Bloody
Foreland

Glasgow

Clyde

North Channel

Belfast

IRELAND

Liverpool

September 3, 1939, when the outward-bound liner *Athenia* was sunk by a German U-boat. By the end of 1939, 114 British and neutral ships, totalling 420,000 tons, had been sunk, among them the carrier *Courageous* and the battleship *Royal Oak*, which was sunk in Scapa Flow by the German submarine U-47 in a daring night raid.

In the meantime Germany's surface warships had not been fulfilling expectations: in December the splendid pocket battleship *Graf Spee* was run to earth in the mouth of the River Plate and scuttled; her sister

ship *Deutschland* (later *Lützow*) made little impression in her North Atlantic raiding operations; and the two battle-cruisers *Scharnhorst* and *Gneisenau* made only one brief sortie.

Having started the war with a U-boat force numbering only fifty-six craft, the German *Kriegsmarine* saw this number steadily growing, while Allied convoys remained desperately short of escorts. The situation was somewhat relieved by the entry into service in the spring of 1940 of the first corvettes, but the danger to Allied shipping was doubled by the fall of France in June 1940. Now, of

A map showing the approaches to the North Channel used by convoys bound for England. It was in this area that the U-boats operated in autumn 1940 and winter 1940–41, precipitating the first convoy battles.

course, the English Channel was no longer safe, and the Atlantic shipping routes too were soon threatened by the new submarine bases established by the Germans at Brest, Lorient and other points of France's Atlantic seaboard. Ocean-going U-boats could now operate deeper into the Atlantic than destroyer escorts on outward convoys, and Dönitz was not slow to take advantage of this weak spot in the convoy system.

The only route now open to convoys to and from Britain was by way of the north-western approaches — round the north of Ireland — but even that route lay open to attack from long-range Focke-Wulf Kondor

◄
The magnificent pocket battleship *Graf Spee*, faster than a battleship and more heavily armed than a cruiser. Her ocean-raiding career was abruptly ended in 1939.

▲
The heavy cruiser *Exeter*, which bore the brunt of *Graf Spee*'s big guns in the River Plate engagement. Sailors and dockyard workers cheer her as she arrives at Plymouth, February 15, 1940.

►
Allied shipping falls victim to marauding U-boats in the Atlantic.

bombers based in Norway and France. In September 1940 Churchill, desperate to strengthen the numbers of convoy escorts, made a Lend-Lease agreement with Roosevelt under the terms of which Britain got the use of fifty First World War four-stacker destroyers from the US naval reserve in exchange for bases on the far side of the Atlantic, but still there were too few escorts, and in October 1940 U-boats sank a total of 350,000 tons of shipping, the highest figure so far.

Bad weather brought a lull in the battle during the winter of 1940–41, but in the spring Dönitz renewed the offensive with a devastating new tactic. He began to deploy teams of submarines in what were termed 'wolf packs'. The members of the

◄
Admiral Erich Raeder, commander-in-chief of the *Kriegsmarine*. He pinned his hopes on his mighty surface ships at the expense of the development of the U-boat arm.

▼
The armed merchant cruiser *Jervis Bay*, sunk by the pocket battleship *Admiral Scheer* while escorting an Atlantic convoy of thirty-eight ships. Leaving the convoy to scatter, *Jervis Bay* closed with the enemy and fought till she sank. By thus sacrificing herself she saved the convoy.

► The 42,000-ton battle-cruiser *Hood*, largest ship in the Royal Navy, sank within minutes of engaging the German battleship *Bismarck* in May 1941. All but a handful of her crew were lost. *Bismarck*'s shell penetrated her magazine, which blew up. The fact that the shell was able to do this was due to a deficiency in design which had caused British battle-cruisers in the First World War to suffer the same devastating fate. *Hood*'s vulnerability to long-range, plunging fire, which had destroyed her predecessors, remained uncured.

►▼ The pride of the *Kriegsmarine*, the battleship *Bismarck*, sank after a long pursuit and an appalling pounding in May 1941, on her first and last mission.

▲
Photographed from her accompanying cruiser *Prinz Eugen*, *Bismarck* fires into the night at her pursuers.

▶
A scene from early in the war, before the entry of the United States. A German U-boat lies off the US freighter *Wacosta*, first US ship to be stopped by a U-boat in the Atlantic. The U-boat fired a shell across the ship's bows, whereupon a lifeboat was lowered and the U-boat captain was taken on a search of the ship.

A U-boat makes a rendezvous with a heavy cruiser in the Atlantic.

pack would spread out and patrol a wide area until one of them picked up a convoy. This submarine would then summon the others by wireless, and when they had assembled, the pack would make a surface attack on the convoy by night. Their speed on the surface exceeded that of most of the convoy escorts, but what was more important was that the escorts' Asdic apparatus was unable to detect their presence. The wolf packs would attack night after night, withdrawing for the daylight hours, and had a devastating effect, but fortunately

Dönitz did not have enough of them. Nevertheless in March 1941, U-boats, surface raiders (the pocket battleship *Admiral Scheer* and the heavy cruisers *Scharnhorst* and *Gneisenau*), and aircraft claimed between them over 500,000 tons of Allied shipping.

In May of the same year one of the last great ship-to-ship engagements took place. The magnificent new German battleship *Bismarck*, in company with the new cruiser *Prinz Eugen*, steamed out into the Atlantic in search of prey. They were soon spotted, and the British battle-cruiser

▲
U-boat chief Admiral Dönitz photographed
with his flotilla commanders and
successful U-boat captains.
▶

A U-boat crewman goes over the side in
mid-Atlantic to attend to a propeller fault.
Running repairs had to be carried out in
far from ideal conditions.

Hood and battleship *Prince of Wales* put out to intercept them. On May 24 they were brought to battle, and the mighty 42,000-ton *Hood*, packing eight 15-inch guns, was blown up by the *Bismarck*'s first salvo, while the *Prince of Wales* sustained damage sufficient to cause her to break off shortly afterwards. *Bismarck* had been hit twice by the *Prince of Wales* and had a fuel leak, so she turned to make for a French Atlantic port, but after repeated attacks by British carrier-borne torpedo-bombers (only one of which achieved a hit, and that a slight one), she gave her attackers the slip. Over a day later

she was spotted again, and was once more attacked by torpedo-bombers. This time she received two hits, one of which jammed her rudders. Now uncontrollable but seemingly unsinkable, she was first pounded by shells from the battleships *Rodney* and *King George V*, then finally torpedoed by the *Dorsetshire* before she slipped beneath the waves. *Prinz Eugen*, which had earlier parted company with *Bismarck*, later put safely into Brest, but the destruction of *Bismarck* spelled the end of Germany's efforts to win the Battle of the Atlantic with surface warships.

Earlier, in March 1941, the Lend-

▼
U-boat crewmen huddle by the conning-tower as their ship, straddled by bombs from a US carrier-borne aircraft, sinks.

An aircraft from RAF Coastal Command patrols overhead as a convoy steams on. ▼

A photograph taken from the corvette *Widgeon*, which has just picked up a convoy. ▶

Lease Bill had been signed. Under its terms Britain was able to place orders for weapons and supplies without immediate payment. This, together with the United States' unilateral extension of the so-called 'Security Zone' off her eastern seaboard (within which U-boats had to respect the neutrality of American shipping) and her decision to furnish an Atlantic support group for Allied shipping, indicated to the Germans that the Americans were becoming rather less than neutral. These measures, however, considerably improved the Allied convoys' chances in the Atlantic, and when the Royal Canadian Navy began to provide escorts as far as south of Iceland, a continuous transatlantic escort system at last came into being.

Towards the end of 1941, prospects seemed to be brightening, although there was still a shortage of long-range aircraft for convoy duties, and the U-boats, now being produced with welded pressure hulls in place of plated and riveted ones, were becoming harder to sink. Events were to take a decisive turn for the worse, however. After America's entry into the war in response to the bombing of Pearl Harbor in December 1941, the Security Zone ceased to exist. Dönitz was not slow to appreciate that he could now make a killing off the eastern seaboard of America, and the figures of 500,000 tons sunk in February 1942 and 700,000 tons in June bear witness to the success of this new offensive. By August 1942 more than 300 U-boats were in service, and despite the introduction of 10-centimetre radar sets and HFDF equipment (which could pinpoint a U-boat by its wireless transmissions), the Allies suffered the loss of 729,000 tons in November.

HMS *Pursuer*, an escort carrier, in 1944. A Wildcat squadron is flying overhead and a squadron of Avengers are on her deck.

An Avenger takes off from *Pursuer*'s flight deck.

By early 1943, however, the Allies had at last evolved what proved to be a truly effective counterattack system, and perhaps more important, very long-range Liberator aircraft at last became available for extensive convoy duties. Although 627,000 tons of shipping was lost in March, the figures for April and May showed a progressive and dramatic decline. By May, Dönitz reckoned that out of every three U-boats he had at sea he stood to lose one, and on May 23, seeing that he could not withstand such losses for long, he ordered his U-boats to withdraw from the North Atlantic.

Although the campaign continued until the end of the war, by July 1943 buildings of new merchant ships had at last begun to exceed losses, and the battle was won.

▲
A convoy photographed from an RAF Sunderland. The combination of long-range shore-based aircraft and aircraft from small escort carriers did much to provide adequate protection against U-boats.

◄
Escort carriers pitching in a heavy Atlantic swell.

The Soft Underbelly:
Sicily and Italy 1943-45

Several factors contributed to the Allies' decision to invade Sicily and Italy. They wanted to secure their communications in the Mediterranean; to form a second front, as requested by Stalin, that would divert German forces from the Russian front; and to keep up pressure on the Italians and Germans so that preparations for the planned landings in Normandy could be completed.

After the final victory in North Africa, the Americans had urged that landings in Normandy should follow as soon as possible, but Churchill was convinced that a swift blow aimed at what he called 'the soft underbelly' of Europe could have a decisive effect, and plans for the Italian campaign went ahead. The

◄◄
A Canadian Navy landing-craft disgorges its contents on a Sicilian beach at the start of the Sicilian campaign.

◄
Allied paratroops drop down on Sicily on July 9, 1943. The seaborne landings followed next day.
◄▼
Seaforth Highlanders wade ashore from a landing-craft.
▶
General Montgomery with Lord Louis Mountbatten in Sicily after the landings.
▶▼
Mopping-up operations in a Sicilian town on a hot afternoon. There was little Italian resistance on the island.

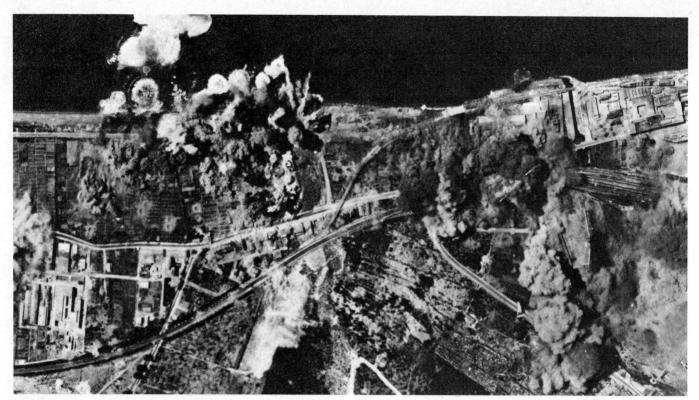

Supreme Commander of operations was Eisenhower, with Alexander as his deputy, while the British and American armies involved were commanded by Montgomery and Patton respectively.

The campaign eventually succeeded, albeit belatedly and with less significant consequences than had been desired. Among the reasons for its success in the initial phases were the fact that Hitler and Mussolini had sent too many troops to North Africa in the closing stages of that campaign, and then failed to evacuate them back to Italy; Mussolini's reluctance to accept German help in the defence of Italy; and the very extent of the coastlines, stretching from Greece to the Atlantic, that Hitler had to defend.

Operations started with an assault on Sicily on July 9, 1943, by British and American airborne troops. Unfortunately the weather was stormy and the assault was dispersed, many gliders carrying troops ending up in the sea, but the unintentionally scattered nature of the attack had the happy effect of causing confusion among the defenders.

The main seaborne assault began on the following day, July 10. British forces under Montgomery landed on Sicily's south-east corner, while Patton's American army landed on the south coast some twenty miles to the west. Italian resistance to the landings was fairly easily overcome, and both forces were soon pushing inland. Montgomery headed up the

◀ American bombs explode in and off Salerno prior to the landings there by the US 5th Army under Mark Clark.

◀▼ Mark Clark seated on a landing-craft as it heads for a Salerno beach. The Germans made the landings extremely difficult.

▼ A convoy of Italian prisoners in the north of Sicily. When this picture was taken, Patton was not far from Messina.

▼▼ British soldiers crouch behind a wall, watching for stray enemy troops.

east coast towards Messina, but found his way effectively blocked by German troops, and was forced to make a difficult and time-consuming detour westwards through the mountainous country round Mount Etna before resuming his drive towards

Messina. Patton, in the meantime, took his forces round the west coast and then headed eastwards, taking Palermo. American troops were the first to enter Messina, on August 17, by which time the remaining German and Italian forces had effected a withdrawal across the Straits to Italy.

The fall of Sicily finally destroyed the Italian people's will to continue their part in the war. Mussolini was deposed by a coup d'état and his Fascist régime instantly collapsed. On September 3, the day on which Montgomery's 8th Army landed on the toe of Italy, the Italians signed an armistice with the Allies. However, the Germans were determined to fight on. Already German troops were moving into Italy and southwards – Hitler had not failed to anticipate the collapse of Italian resistance.

The landings in the south of Italy, at the toe and heel, met with little resistance. Taranto was taken on September 9 and the useful port of

◄
Canadian troops doing some 'house-cleaning' and sniper-hunting in the town of Ortona, December 1943.

◄▼
Infantrymen leaving a landing-craft on the beach at Anzio.

▲
DUKW's on ship-to-shore ferry duties at Anzio.

►
A German shell sends a column of water into the air alongside a DUKW off the Anzio beachhead.

Bari on September 22, and British forces moved steadily, if slowly, northward. But this was a diversionary operation, designed to draw the German forces, for the main landings were to take place at Salerno, on the west coast, followed up by a drive towards Rome. On September 9 General Mark Clark's 9th Army landed at Salerno, to be met by German resistance so strong that at one point Clark was considering withdrawing from the beaches altogether. The Germans had not been deceived by the landings in the south, and fought furiously to stop the establishment of a bridgehead and subsequent incursions inland, but, aided by a highly effective barrage from heavy naval guns offshore (including the devastating 15-inch guns of the British battleships *Warspite* and *Valiant*), Clark's forces were able to break through, and by the first week of October had reached the River Volturno, north of Naples, which was now in Allied hands. Here the Germans held them for a while before

▼
A US 5th Army 155-mm gun opens fire on German positions from the Anzio beachhead. The struggle to retain the beachhead was tough.

withdrawing to the Gustav line, a defensive barrier which the German Commander, Field-Marshal Kesselring, had swiftly established slightly further north. The crucial stronghold on this line, which ran from the west to the east coast, was Monte Cassino, guarding the vital Route 6 leading to Rome. Here the Allied advance was halted, and a stalemate ensued that was to last until the spring of 1944. The Allies launched assaults at various points in the line in November and December, but they all broke down, having sustained heavy casualties.

The next major effort to dislodge the Germans from their positions came in January 1944. On January 12 a major assault was launched on the Cassino stronghold and other points along the Gustav line, and on January 22 Allied forces made a landing at Anzio, behind the Gustav line on the west coast. The plan was for the Anzio force to attack Cassino from the rear and thus assist a breakthrough by the forces moving

Italian Theatre of War

ITALY

CORSICA

Valmontone
Rome
Alban Hills
Velletri
Pescara
Garigliano
Rapido
Ortona
Moletta
Campoleone
Nettuno
Sangro
Carocetto
Liri
Lepini Mountains
Anzio
Cisterna
Albano
Monte Cassino
Pontine Marshes
Terracina
Naples
Gaeta
Salerno
Ischia
Capri

SARDINIA

Palermo
Messina

SICILY

Tunis

TUNISIA

At the end of May 1944 the Anzio force
finally broke out of its beachhead. The
picture shows a carrier platoon awaiting
orders to carry ammunition forward during
the offensive.

150

on Cassino from the south. However, the move misfired. The attack on Cassino was beaten off and the Anzio force, surrounded by the Germans, was pushed back towards the sea, though it managed to hold out until the eventual breakthrough at Cassino in May.

On May 11, after months of preparation, the Allies launched a final assault on the Gustav line. The attacking front was no less than thirteen miles wide, and this tactic took the Germans by surprise. On May 18 the Polish Corps captured the Cassino stronghold and drove the German defenders out of the rubble of the ruined monastery, and on May 23 the Germans abandoned the Gustav line. Mark Clark's Anzio force was now able to break out of its long-defended bridgehead, and it was Alexander's intention that it should cut across eastwards to encircle the German forces now leaving the Gustav line. Clark, however, had other ideas. Detaching only one division to attempt the encirclement, he wheeled northwards with four divisions and headed for Rome, which his forces entered on June 4, Kesselring having declared it an open city rather than see it destroyed in battle.

Two days after the entry into Rome, on June 6, the Allied invasion of Normandy began. The Italian campaign had succeeded only to a

▼
The devastation of the Cassino battle zone, seen from the Allied lines in March 1944, before the capture of the stronghold in May.

The shattered town of Cassino after the battle.

After months of fighting, this was all that remained of the medieval monastery of Monte Cassino in May 1944.

154

◀
8th Army troops and tanks advance towards the Gothic line in the late summer of 1944.

◀▼
Tanks of the 5th Army move up to attack the Gothic line, where the Germans held the Allies until the end of April 1945.

▼
Winter on the Gothic line, 1944–45.

limited degree in its objective of disabling Hitler from building up his strength in northern France, and in itself it had so far yielded disappointing results.

The events that succeeded the capture of Rome did nothing to relieve the Allies' disappointment. Kesselring's forces held up the advance northwards every inch of the way, and though Alexander had aimed to reach the Germans' next defensive line, the Gothic line, by August 15, his offensive at the

Gothic line did not open until August 25. Very slow progress was made, and after months of fighting the offensive petered out around Christmas 1944. The Allies now went on to the defensive in order to build up strength for a major thrust in the spring. This took place in mid-April, and by the end of the month, with the line pierced and most of the German forces surrounded, resistance was at an end. On May 2 the Germans surrendered.

155

Retreat in Russia

◄◄
Russian tanks cover an infantry advance in a Polish forest as the drive westwards continues.

The winter of 1941 saw Hitler's forces checked outside Moscow and his advance into Russia at a halt. He now planned a new offensive for the spring of 1942. In the north he would strike again at Leningrad, but the major offensive would come in the south, where it was necessary to secure the oilfields of the Caucasus to fuel Germany's war effort. This drive was to be accompanied and protected by a flanking move south-eastwards to Stalingrad which, if successful, would cut off any Russian forces heading for the Caucasus.

It was the Russians, however, who struck first. On May 12, 1942, a large Russian force advanced on

►
February 1942: German troops plod past a wrecked Russian tank.

▼
Abandoned German guns and vehicles litter a road in January 1942.

Kharkov, but the assault was thrown back. By the end of May, General Timoshenko and 240,000 Russian troops had been taken prisoner. With the Russians reeling from this blow, Kleist's 1st Panzer Army broke through the Don-Donetz corridor in June and, pressing on, took the key city of Rostov, cutting off the Russians' oil pipeline from the Caucasus. Kleist's forces now fanned out southwards, but before long fuel shortages and the mountainous country slowed them down, and by October the advance had halted.

In the meantime, General von Paulus and the German 6th Army, driving on down the Don-Donetz

▼ German tanks advancing during the summer of 1942.

corridor, had reached the Don bend near Kalach, only forty miles from Stalingrad, on July 28. On August 23 the attack on Stalingrad, which was finally to toll the knell of the German advance in Russia, was launched. It took the form of a pincer movement by the 6th Army from north-west of the city and the 4th Panzer Army from the south-west. The defenders kept the two arms of the pincer well apart, however, and the Germans responded by launching a direct attack from the west. This combination now produced a semicircular attacking front which began gradually to converge upon the city, becoming tighter and tighter. The Russians were fighting with their backs to the two-mile-wide Volga, and were determined not to give ground. The Germans hurled attack after attack at them, but as the front narrowed it became easier for the Russians to meet an assault from any quarter. In the meantime, the Germans' relentless effort to drive home the assault was draining away their reserves of men and machines, and their flanking forces grew increasingly weak.

In September the fighting moved into the suburbs. The city had been pounded into rubble by German bombardment, but its citizens and soldiers would not give way. They constructed makeshift barricades in the wreckage-strewn streets and manned the ruined houses. In the bitter street fighting that raged from now on, the Germans found themselves measuring their forward progress in inches. The attack on Stalingrad had become a nightmare battle of attrition, but it was clear that the Russian defenders were losing ground. A counterstroke was needed, and soon it came.

On November 19 and 20, 1942, two Russian spearheads drove westwards from north and south of the city, then turned inwards, neatly and comprehensively encircling von Paulus's exhausted army. This classic move, planned by Generals Zhukov, Vasilevsky and Voronov, was com-

◀
Russian infantry leap from tanks to meet the advancing Germans outside Stalingrad.

◀▼
A Russian mortar is dragged hurriedly up to the front line under fire.

▼
A Red Army soldier prepares to hurl a grenade at a German position in the suburbs of Stalingrad.

▲▲
An expansive gesture from Goering, while Mussolini and Hitler listen, at the Führer's headquarters in East Prussia. Albert Speer compared these barbed-wire compounds deep in the gloomy Prussian forest to a prison. In this atmosphere Hitler and entourage gradually lost touch with reality.

▲
A handful of Stalingrad's defenders advance cautiously over rubble-strewn ground in the ruins of the city.

pleted by November 23, and was accompanied by a wider westward encirclement intended to parry any possible German thrust to relieve the trapped army. Von Paulus's appeal to Hitler for permission to attempt a withdrawal from the city was summarily rejected, but Manstein was instructed to mount a relief operation. In mid-December Manstein's hastily assembled Army Group Don moved up from a southerly direction in a bid to join up with von Paulus's 6th Army, and penetrated

to within thirty miles of its objective, but was then brought to a halt by the Russians.

The fate of the 6th Army was now sealed, and a huge Russian counter-offensive gathered momentum. Suddenly, their ascendancy removed, German forces were on the retreat. Russian forces swept the Germans from the Don-Donetz corridor, thus threatening to cut off their forces in the Caucasus. In a desperate race to get out before the gap was closed, German troops poured out of the

▶
Russians defending the Krasny Oktyabr factory on the alert as aircraft pass overhead.

▼
German soldiers pick their way through the wreckage in a shattered Stalingrad factory. Nothing that fell into German hands was of any use.

▲
A Russian field-gun firing at German positions in the ruins of the Krasny Oktyabr plant. As winter deepened, the Russians fought back with ever greater effect.

◄
A tight-lipped von Paulus at the Russian headquarters after his surrender at Stalingrad.

►
After the Russian encirclement of Stalingrad, German forces in the Caucasus were nearly cut off. The picture shows Russian troops in trenches in the Caucasus as the Germans retreat northwards.

Russian tanks advance towards the front inside the Kursk salient in July 1943. Hitler aimed to cut off Russian forces in the salient with a pincer movement at its flanks.

Caucasus via Rostov, slipping out as the door clanged shut at the end of January 1943.

On January 10 the Russians had launched a massive encircling attack on the army trapped at Stalingrad, and finally, in spite of Hitler's instructions to fight to the death, von Paulus surrendered on January 31. Coming close on the precipitate withdrawal from the Caucasus, the surrender at Stalingrad, in which 92,000 Germans gave themselves up, saw Germany's Russian ambitions in pieces, while, for the German people, the name of Stalingrad from then on symbolised doom and folly. In the north, too, Germany suffered a reverse, and Hitler a blow to his pride, when Russian forces were at last able to punch a hole through the circle of German positions round Leningrad and bring supplies into the beleaguered city, though another year was to pass before the siege was finally broken.

February 1943 saw the continuation of Russian offensives in different parts of the southern sector, culminating in a sweep southwards at the end of the month. This represented another attempt to cut off

German forces in the south, but a German counterstroke re-established their position to a limited degree, and this was followed by a three-month pause. During this period Hitler concentrated on building up and refitting his army in preparation for a new offensive.

He had little doubt about what its objective should be—indeed the objective, the inviting bulge of the Kursk salient, was as obvious to the Russians as it was to him. He planned to bite off the bulge and encircle the Russian forces in it with another classic envelopment by Manstein's army from the north and von Kluge's from the south.

The operation began on July 5, but neither of the two attacking forces was able to achieve a decisive penetration. The Russians had laid deep minefields in the way and had established strong defensive positions in anticipation of Hitler's moves. After a week it became plain to Manstein and von Kluge that their losses were running at a rate which they could not sustain, and von Kluge began to pull out. The Russians now countered with a thrust at the adjoining German-held Orel salient

▲
German forces move up towards Kursk before the battle. Around 3,000 tanks were involved on both sides, Hitler throwing in almost all the armour available on the Eastern Front.

▶▲
A German soldier jumps off a blazing tank during the Kursk battle. After a week the Germans pulled out.

▶
Red Army soldiers inspect two Tiger tanks knocked out at Kursk.

◀ The Russians took Kiev in November 1943. A subsequent offensive aimed at cutting off the Russians' Kiev bulge failed. The picture shows a German soldier amidst the ruins of a blazing town in the sector during the offensive.

▶ The great Russian commander Marshal Zhukov, instrumental in the German collapse at Stalingrad, who led the drive westwards after the battle of the Kiev bulge.

▼ Russian rocket launchers in the Carpathians in 1944.

on July 12, and squeezed the Germans backwards. The retreating forces resisted all the way, but when they tried to hold on to positions east of the Dnieper, their front line had worn so thin from losses in continuous fighting that they failed. Had they conducted a rapid retreat after the collapse of their positions around Orel, they might have been able to dig in east of the Dnieper and halt the Russian advance.

On November 6 the Germans lost the Vistula. They had travelled so far, and so fast, that their communications and lines of supply had become overstretched, allowing the Germans to rally. Here the line stabilised for a while. At the end of August, Russian forces in the southern sector swept through Rumania, trapping the German 6th Army, twenty divisions being lost. Now the Russian left wing wheeled upwards through Eastern Europe, reaching Budapest in November. Here they were baulked

▼ Russian artillery bombards German positions in East Prussia at the beginning of 1945.

Kiev, and in the ensuing winter and spring the Russian advance accelerated in both northern and southern sectors. In January 1944 Leningrad was liberated, and in April the Crimea. In June the Russians launched an offensive with 166 divisions north of the Pripet marshes, timed to coincide with the Normandy invasions and thus bring maximum pressure to bear on all fronts. In a pincer movement on Minsk, a vital rail and communications centre, they trapped 100,000 Germans.

In August, Russian forces reached

by German and Hungarian forces.

When 1944 drew to a close, the Russian front line stretched from the eastern frontier of East Prussia via Warsaw and Budapest to Lake Balaton. In January 1945 they launched a new offensive which pierced the line in all sectors, and by the end of February the armies of the centre had reached the Oder-Neisse line, inside Germany, where the Germans managed, for a few short months, to hold them, at the expense of their western defences. The end was not far off.

▶ A Red Army column rumbles past dead Germans and abandoned equipment in a German town in January 1945.

172

Normandy and the Liberation of France

At their conference in Tehran in November 1943 Churchill, Roosevelt and Stalin had agreed on the timing of the invasion of France. Stalin, never particularly happy about the validity of the Allies' Italian campaign as a second front, was finally to have the second front that he had long been advocating: pressure on the Germans from the west to match the pressure which, since his armies' victory at Stalingrad, he had been so relentlessly applying. For the Allies, too, the invasion of France represented the crowning effort to smash Hitler's Germany, for which the Italian campaign gave them time to plan, while at the same time diverting and eating up Hitler's resources.

Hitler, for his part, had not failed to anticipate the likelihood of an

◄◄

A Normandy beachhead after the landings. A line of merchant ships has been scuttled offshore to form a breakwater within which ships may unload supplies on to landing-craft for ferrying to the shore.

▲

The leaders of the Allied forces prepare for the liberation of Europe in London in February 1944. Seated: Air Chief Marshal Tedder (Deputy Supreme Commander), General Eisenhower (Supreme Commander), General Montgomery (British Forces). Standing: Lieutenant-General Bradley (US Forces), Admiral Ramsay (Navy), Air Chief Marshal Leigh Mallory (Air Commander-in-Chief), Lieutenant-General Bedell Smith (Chief of Staff).

▶

A tank trap 150 yards behind a Normandy beach, part of the Atlantic Wall defences.

◄ Hitler in discussion with General Sepp
Dietrich in the operations room of his
headquarters in East Prussia.
▼ American troops and vehicles waiting to
embark for the invasion of France.

invasion of France, and had detailed Rommel to defend the coastline from Holland to Brittany. Von Rundstedt, as supreme commander in France, was to control operations and maintain mobile reserves in Rommel's rear. Tank traps, pillboxes, and other fortifications were erected along the coast, forming the Atlantic Wall, but Hitler's preparations were hampered by lack of intelligence as to where the blow would fall.

On the night of June 5–6 three Allied airborne divisions were dropped over Normandy: two US divisions at the base of the Cotentin peninsula, and one British division further east, near Caen. Their task was to secure bridges and other vital communications points behind the coastline in order to delay the arrival of German

reinforcements. The Germans were completely unprepared for this move: firstly the weather was so stormy that they considered an attack impossible; secondly they had expected landings in the Calais-Dieppe area (which contained the launching sites of the V-weapons); and thirdly none of the senior German commanders in the area was available. This combination of circumstances meant that, for the most part, the Normandy invasion got off to a good start. With the paratroops' objectives achieved, 150,000 men, carried by 2,700 vessels, began to land next day, supported by a heavy aerial and naval bombardment. The landings on the five designated beaches were accomplished with varying degrees of difficulty: of the two American beaches in the west,

▲
General Eisenhower chats with paratroopers before they are dropped in Normandy in the first stage of the invasion. Their task was to secure important communications points inland.

▶
Members of an American landing party carry dripping comrades ashore from a life-raft after their landing-craft was sunk.

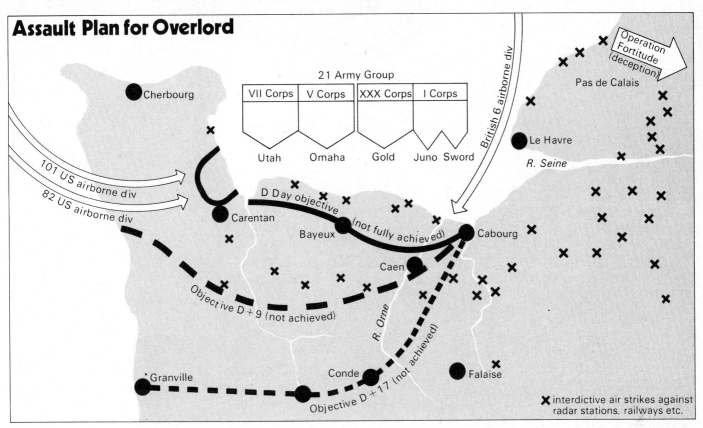

Assault Plan for Overlord

Cherbourg

21 Army Group

VII Corps	V Corps	XXX Corps	I Corps
Utah	Omaha	Gold	Juno Sword

101 US airborne div

82 US airborne div

British 6 airborne div

Operation Fortitude (deception)

Pas de Calais

Le Havre

R. Seine

D Day objective

Carentan

Bayeux

(not fully achieved)

Cabourg

Caen

R. Orne

Objective D+9 (not achieved)

Granville

Conde

Objective D+17 (not achieved)

Falaise

✕ interdictive air strikes against radar stations, railways etc.

A crowded scene on one of the beaches after landing as British troops wait to go forward.

A Mulberry harbour off the Normandy coast, with unloading in process. Although they represented a considerable technical achievement, gales soon put one out of action and crippled the other.

US troops move out of their Normandy beachhead. Traffic congestion was a problem throughout the initial stages of the invasion.

Utah presented a happier picture, and a beachhead was soon successfully established; but on Omaha the story was different. Many of the amphibious tanks sank before reaching the shore; the German forces in the area were strong and on stand-to; and there was severe congestion, cramping movement and manœuvre, on the beach. On the British and Canadian beaches further east, Gold, Juno and Sword, the landings went smoothly, aided by such devices as tanks equipped with revolving flails to clear a path through minefields.

Apart from the fighting at Omaha, the Germans mounted no real counterattack. They had too few men in the area, too few tanks, and the Luftwaffe was completely dominated by the RAF. Rommel had always advocated crushing any invasion on the beaches, before it could gain a toehold, but von Rundstedt did not agree. In any event, his superiors on Hitler's staff persisted in the belief that the Normandy landings were a decoy, and that the main invasion was to be expected elsewhere. Therefore the troops were held back.

In these conditions the invading forces soon established a firm footing, and men and machines continued to pour in. After twenty days

A US Liberator bomber turns away after bombing the airfield at St Dizier in northern France. The Allied air forces completely dominated the Luftwaffe during the liberation.

US infantrymen, firing a bazooka, achieve a hit on a German tank in a French town.

◄
As American tanks and vehicles move southwards, an ammunition-carrying truck is blown up by a German mortar bomb.

▼
Led by a Sherman, tanks squeeze through the streets of a town in Normandy, while townspeople look on.

Hitler's HQ at Rastenburg in East Prussia after the bomb plot against his life on July 20, 1944. Several generals were implicated in the conspiracy. Hitler escaped with slight injuries.

A huge pall of smoke rises from the Falaise pocket, in which thousands of trapped Germans were mercilessly bombarded; 50,000 of them were encircled and taken prisoner.

Paris, August 1944. The tricolour flies proudly on a German tank captured in a street battle. Resistance fighters and Free French troops fought alongside each other during the liberation.

more than a million men were ashore, and artificial harbours were constructed to facilitate the unloading of the enormous quantities of stores involved. These harbours were of two types: Gooseberry harbours, made up of lines of scuttled merchant ships; and Mulberry harbours, made of huge prefabricated concrete sections which were towed into position and then sunk. Additionally, a flexible pipeline, known as Pluto, was laid across the Channel to ensure a steady supply of motor fuel.

Soon the armies began to advance inland from the beaches. Patton and the US 3rd Army pushed south through St Lo, then divided, one force sweeping south-westwards into Brittany to mop up German forces there, the other driving south and east towards Paris. Meanwhile the British and Canadians were held by the Germans round Caen. Hitler saw in this situation a chance to split the

invading forces in half by punching through to Avranches on the west coast and thus cutting Patton's army off from the Allied forces in the north. This counterattack by four panzer divisions was contained, and in a short time turned into a resounding defeat. Patton swung northwards, and the Canadians pressed southwards, aiming to take the Germans in the rear, but the Canadians, meeting strong resistance, were unable to move as fast as Patton's army, and Patton was ordered to halt. Reluctantly he did so, but as a result the attempted envelopment failed. Nevertheless, the German troops in the Falaise pocket suffered a terrible pounding, and though some of them were able to withdraw towards Paris, 50,000 were taken prisoner.

On August 19 French underground forces rose against the Germans in Paris, and on August 25, following the surrender of the German commander, General de Gaulle proclaimed the liberation of the city by parading down the Champs-Elysées. The first Allied forces to enter the city had been the Free French under General Leclerc, arriving to support the underground fighters.

In the meantime the Allied armies were racing across France on a broad front, with Montgomery's 21st Army Group advancing along the north coast, taking Le Havre, Boulogne, Calais and Dunkirk, and Patton's 3rd Army driving eastwards

▼ General de Gaulle marches down the Champs-Elysées after the liberation of Paris, with cheering Parisians lining his route.

through the middle. Montgomery advocated a single concentrated thrust at Germany's industrial centre, the Ruhr, in the north; Patton wanted to drive to the Rhine south of Frankfurt. There was insufficient fuel and transport to sustain both. Eisenhower was faced with a tricky decision: which course, or which combination of them, would defeat Germany soonest? He compromised. Montgomery could have the lion's share till he had secured Belgium and therefore his approaches to Germany.

▶ Troops keep watch outside Arnhem, where there was a bitter struggle resulting in a British withdrawal.

Then the eastward thrust north and south of the Ardennes would be resumed. Patton, disgusted, announced his intention to press on till his vehicles ran out of fuel, which they did at the Meuse on August 31. On September 3 Montgomery's forces took Brussels, and on September 4 Antwerp. Now Patton got his share of fuel, but the pause in his advance had given the Germans time to assemble some opposition, and he was blocked at Metz.

The next stage in Montgomery's operations in the north opened on September 17, when airborne landings took place aimed at securing the Rhine bridge at Arnhem and the bridges over the Maas and Waal at Eindhoven and Nijmegen. The US paratroopers at Eindhoven and Nijmegen successfully achieved their objectives, but the British at Arnhem fared badly. The British 2nd Army, which was to march north to join up with them, was checked, and after nine days of constant fighting, without support, those paratroopers who had escaped death, injury or capture withdrew. Of 10,000 men dropped, only 2,000 returned.

Now the advance on all fronts petered out. All the while the Germans had been assembling a defensive line and thickening it up, and even a combined Allied offensive all along the front in November made little progress. Hitler's counter-offensive at the end of the year was to keep the Allies at bay even longer.

▼ Paratroops drop into Holland on September 17, 1944.

▲
German prisoners captured at Nijmegen.
The bridge at Nijmegen was one of the
objectives of the airborne invasion, and
was successfully secured.
◀
B-17 bombers attacking a railway bridge in
Hungary, October 1944. This attack was
one of many by Mediterranean-based
aircraft in support of the advancing
Russians.

Recovery in the Pacific

US Marines wade to their tents after a torrential downpour on Guadalcanal. The struggle for this island lasted six months and saw six major engagements at sea as well as ceaseless fighting ashore.

December 1941 had seen the Japanese attack on Pearl Harbor, and the ensuing months witnessed the rapid spread of Japanese power in the Pacific and South East Asia. It was not until April 1942 that the Americans struck back. On April 18, eighteen B-52 Mitchell bombers took off from US aircraft carriers in the Pacific and dropped their bombs on Tokyo. This exploit, the Tokyo Raid, gave a sizeable boost to American morale, and prompted the Japanese high command to look for ways of destroying the US Fleet so that the raid would not be repeated. They decided to attack the island of Mid-way, a move which they thought would draw the US Navy to contest their assault, for a Japanese presence

▲
Emperor Hirohito of Japan inspects bomb damage in Tokyo. The first American raid on the city came in April 1942, and reinforced Japanese intentions to complete the destruction of the US Fleet at Midway.
▶
Admiral Chester W. Nimitz (right), commander-in-chief of the Pacific Fleet.

194

Admiral Yamamoto, commander-in-chief of the Japanese Combined Fleet.
▼
Smoke billows from the carrier *Lexington* following an attack by Japanese dive- and torpedo-bombers at Coral Sea. In the foreground the cruiser *Minneapolis* takes off *Lexington*'s crew.

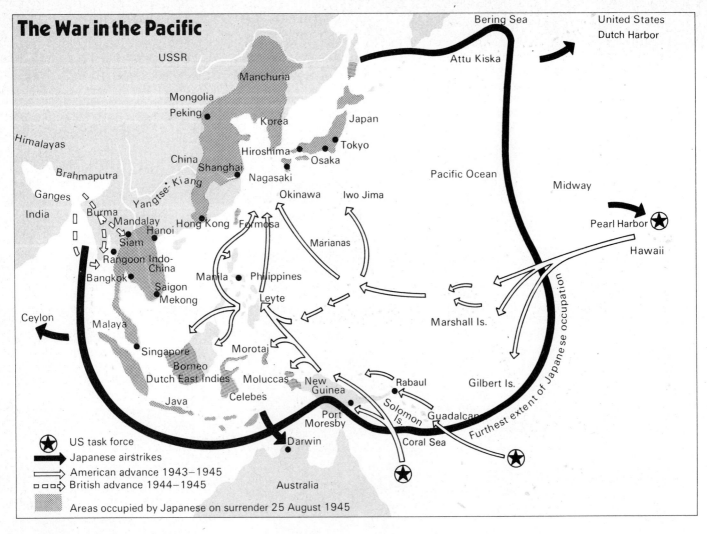

The War in the Pacific

USSR
Manchuria
Mongolia
Peking
Korea
Japan
Hiroshima
Tokyo
Osaka
China
Shanghai
Nagasaki
Himalayas
Brahmaputra
Yangtse-Kiang
Okinawa
Iwo Jima
Pacific Ocean
Midway
Ganges
India
Burma
Mandalay
Hanoi
Hong Kong
Formosa
Marianas
Pearl Harbor
Siam
Hawaii
Rangoon Indo-China
Bangkok
Manila
Philippines
Saigon
Leyte
Mekong
Ceylon
Marshall Is.
Malaya
Singapore
Morotai
Borneo
Dutch East Indies
Moluccas
New Guinea
Rabaul
Gilbert Is.
Java
Celebes
Port Moresby
Solomon Is.
Guadalcanal
Darwin
Coral Sea
Bering Sea
Attu Kiska
United States
Dutch Harbor
Furthest extent of Japanese occupation
Australia

⍟ US task force
➤ Japanese airstrikes
⇨ American advance 1943–1945
▢▢▢⇨ British advance 1944–1945
▨ Areas occupied by Japanese on surrender 25 August 1945

on Midway could threaten the American base at Hawaii. The attack on Midway would be a diversion which they hoped successfully to accommodate during a major thrust southeastwards through the Solomons which aimed at cutting off sea traffic between the United States and Australia, which was being used as a base for the build-up of Allied strength in the Pacific theatre and as a springboard for offensive operations. US forces in the South West Pacific were commanded by General Douglas MacArthur, while Admiral Chester Nimitz commanded the Pacific Ocean.

The first major confrontation resulting from the Japanese strategy was the Battle of the Coral Sea, which took place on May 8, 1942. The Americans had got wind of Japanese plans, and Nimitz had sent all available ships south to block the Japanese invasions. His battleships had been sunk at Pearl Harbor but he was able to muster the carriers *Yorktown* and *Lexington*, with a cruiser force. The Japanese fielded two carriers, together with cruisers and destroyers. In terms of ships and aircraft the two fleets were closely matched. In the

aerial battle which ensued, the first ever in which neither side's ships saw its opponent's ships, one Japanese carrier, the *Shokaku*, was forced to withdraw through damage, while the *Lexington* was sunk. At the end of the day both sides retired, the outcome undecided, but the Japanese had lost more aircraft than the Americans and their plans to attack and take the key town of Port Moresby in New Guinea had been thwarted.

For the subsequent attack on Midway Island Admiral Yamamoto assembled almost the entire Japanese navy, plus an invasion force. He himself sailed in Japan's new giant battleship, the *Yamato*, 73,000 tons, which mounted nine 18-inch guns. The American naval force which came to meet him numbered only seventy-six ships, including the carriers *Enterprise*, *Hornet* and *Yorktown* (hastily repaired after being damaged in the Coral Sea engagement), against Yamamoto's 200.

On June 4 the Japanese launched an air strike on Midway, unaware that the American fleet was approaching. The first air strike being considered insufficient, the torpedo-bombers waiting on the Japanese

▶▲
Fires blaze aboard *Yorktown*. A subsequent air strike launched from the Japanese carrier *Hiryu* sent her to the bottom.

▶
Pilots and crew of the sinking *Yorktown* prepare to abandon ship.

carriers for instructions to attack the US warships exchanged their torpedoes for bombs. Only now did the Japanese carrier force commander, Admiral Nagumo, receive news of the oncoming American force. With his torpedo-bombers equipped with bombs and many of his fighters out on patrol, his position was weak. However, when the first three waves of American torpedo-bombers arrived, they suffered such devastating losses from AA fire and Japanese fighters that Nagumo felt he had gained the advantage.

His confidence was short-lived. A few minutes later thirty-seven American dive-bombers swooped down and attacked. Three of the Japanese carriers, *Akagi*, *Kaga* and *Soryu*, were knocked out, while the fourth, *Hiryu*, later sank, though not before hitting the *Yorktown* so hard that she had to be abandoned.

For the Japanese, this was a considerable setback. They had lost four aircraft carriers and 330 planes. The Americans, on the other hand, had gained the advantage and a valuable breathing-space.

The Japanese advance in the South West Pacific now slowed down, but they were still making progress in the Solomons and, despite the Coral Sea reverse, which foiled their plans for a seaborne assault on Port Moresby, they continued to threaten the Allied position in New Guinea. On July 21, 1942, a Japanese force landed near Buna, on the north coast of New Guinea's Papuan peninsula, with orders to head overland to Port Moresby on the south coast. Though the terrain was difficult and mountainous, they took Kokoda, half-way across the peninsula, and pressed the Australian defenders back to within thirty miles

US Dauntless dive-bombers fly over the
coral reef surrounding Midway Island.

of Port Moresby before being halted. MacArthur soon assembled Australian and American reinforcements, and before long the Japanese were on the retreat. On November 2, Australian troops reoccupied Kokoda, and on January 21, 1943, Japanese resistance ended near Buna, where the offensive had been launched.

While the battle for Port Moresby was being fought, another was raging on the island of Guadalcanal in the Solomons. After their success at Midway, the Americans decided to take the offensive in the South West Pacific, and plans for the re-establishment of the Allied position were in preparation when reconnaissance aircraft reported, on July 5, 1942, that Japanese forces had moved from the island of Tulagi to Guadalcanal, where they had begun work on an airfield. This would present a future threat from Japanese bombers, the Allied command realised, and the capture of Guadalcanal instantly became a top priority. On August 7, US Marines landed on the island, to find the airfield nearly completed and the Japanese hiding in the jungle. On Tulagi, meanwhile, the Japanese garrison was wiped out.

Despite the initial American success, the Japanese were not slow to retaliate. On August 9 a naval force under Admiral Mikawa, comprising five heavy and two light cruisers and a destroyer, slipped through the Slot (the narrow passage between the two chains of the Solomon Islands) and sank four heavy cruisers and disabled another. This disastrous attack forced the remaining Allied naval force to withdraw, leaving the task of unloading supplies on Guadalcanal unfinished. Forces on the island were left in an isolated position, and had the Japanese decided to capitalise on their newly won advantage, they could have wrought havoc. But they made the mistake of underestimating the strength of the US troops on Guadalcanal (then numbering about 11,000), and instead of sending a powerful force to wipe them out, they shipped a mere 1,500 troops, who were cut to pieces on landing.

When they sent their next consignment, of 2,000 troops, the Japanese laid a trap for the US fleet. The light carrier *Ryujo* and the troop-carrying ships were to act as bait to

▼
Admiral Nagumo, commander of the Japanese carrier strike force at Midway. He refused to leave the bridge of his flagship *Akagi* when it was bombed and set ablaze, and had to be dragged off the doomed vessel by his officers.

▼▼
The Japanese cruiser *Mikuma*, torn apart by American dive-bombers during the general retirement of the Japanese fleet at Midway.

draw the US fleet, as at Midway, while behind them steamed two battleships and two fleet carriers. Fortunately the American intelligence network had provided Admiral Ghormley, commander of forces in the area, with warning of the plan, and he was waiting for the Japanese force when it arrived. In this, the Battle of the Eastern Solomons, on August 24, the Japanese lost the *Ryujo* and seventy aircraft, while the American carrier *Enterprise* sustained some damage. The engagement was inconclusive, however, and both sides withdrew by night.

After this came a lull, but the Japanese stepped up shipments of troops to Guadalcanal aboard destroyers, the run being nicknamed the 'Tokyo Express'. By the beginning of October they had 22,000 men on the island, and in the middle of the month the airfield, known as Henderson Field, was badly knocked about, a large number of American aircraft being destroyed. The fierce fighting which had raged since midsummer in conditions of oppressive heat and humidity was beginning to take its toll, but when the Japanese

▲ A Mitchell B-25 bombing Japanese installations in the southern Solomons following the landings at Guadalcanal on August 7, 1942.

◄ Exhausted US Marines patrol ground surrounding Henderson Field, the vital airstrip, at the height of the fighting on Guadalcanal.

launched a major offensive on October 24, the Marines were able to drive them off by the 26th with heavy losses, their own losses being small.

Meanwhile, Yamamoto had steamed up with a large fleet, expecting to find Henderson Field in Japanese hands. In the confrontation that followed on October 26, the Santa Cruz Islands battle, the US carrier *Hornet* was sunk and the *Enterprise* damaged again. Two Japanese carriers were damaged, but the Japanese suffered the greater loss in aircraft, seventy in all. Their aircraft losses were running at a rate they could not afford, while American air power was being increased.

Nevertheless the Japanese tried again, in two consecutive naval engagements which took place between November 13 and 15. There were losses on both sides, but Japanese losses were heavier. Of a detachment of 11,000 men shipped to reinforce their troops on Guadalcanal, only 4,000 were landed.

On land the Americans had taken the offensive. Japanese supplies and reinforcements were not getting through, and their troops were on reduced rations, but they fought on grimly. By January 1943, however, the Japanese command realised that the end was near. Between February 1 and 7 the Guadalcanal forces were evacuated, leaving the Americans masters of the island.

With Guadalcanal secured, the Allies now faced the task of seizing the rest of the Solomons and the big Japanese base at Rabaul on New Britain. An attack from two directions on Rabaul was proposed, with MacArthur and Ghormley's successor, Admiral Halsey, working together. MacArthur was to secure the Trobriand Islands, the Lae-Salamaua area of New Guinea, and the western point of New Britain (Rabaul lying at the eastern point). For his part Halsey was to secure the rest of the Solomons and Bougainville, which would make a good springboard for an assault on New Britain.

At the end of June 1943 the combined operation was launched. The

▶
The carrier *Wasp* is swept by fire after being torpedoed by Japanese submarines on September 14, 1942, while carrying troops to Guadalcanal.

▶
American troops on Guadalcanal pile up supplies, while exhausted Japanese prisoners squat in the foreground.

Trobriand Islands were easily taken, and in mid-September, after some difficulty, the Lae-Salamaua objective was achieved. Tough resistance was also met in the Solomons, but by mid-August New Georgia had been secured, providing a base for flights to Bougainville. The campaign so far had taken rather longer than expected, and the cost in human lives and material was too great: some rethinking was necessary if the campaign was not to drag on indefinitely. A scheme emerged. The Allies could leapfrog over the most strongly defended Japanese positions and, by isolating them, neutralise them. This was to be the strategy, but in the meantime, in November 1943, the planned landings on Bougainville went ahead.

The Japanese saw an American presence on Bougainville as a serious threat to their main base at Rabaul, and sent a task force to prevent the landings, but Admiral Spruance's US fleet beat it off. Meanwhile, on Bougainville, Halsey was trying to establish a position large enough to accommodate the planned airfield, but there were 55,000 Japanese troops on the island and his efforts to increase the American-held area met strong resistance. Nevertheless, Halsey had succeeded by the end of the year.

The next move was to have been against Rabaul, but a decision was taken to isolate it rather than attack it, particularly as American gains elsewhere had reduced its potential threat. An airfield would be built on the western point of New Britain instead, in order to launch a final offensive against Japanese forces in New Guinea. This plan went ahead. The airfield was built, and by the end of April 1944 the Allies had established a dominant position in New Guinea, with the Japanese in retreat.

With all these objectives attained, with the Admiralty, Marshall and Gilbert Islands also under their belts, and with Rabaul cut off and thus neutralised, the Allies planned their next move – an attack on the Philippines, the scene of defeat in 1941.

▼
The battleship *South Dakota*, which narrowly escaped destruction in one of the savage night engagements during the long struggle for Guadalcanal. Despite having no radar, the Japanese were expert night fighters at sea.

Burma: the Long Road Back

◄◄

A British patrol moving through muddy ground near the Pegu canal.

▼

Japanese occupation forces pass through a Burmese village.

After the withdrawal into India in 1942, the first British attempt to challenge the Japanese position in Burma was the Arakan offensive, which lasted from December 1942 to May 1943. For various reasons this was a dismal flop: the British had inadequate resources to sustain a prolonged offensive or mount a sufficiently large one; the advance proceeded so slowly that the Japanese had plenty of time to send troops to meet it; and Wavell's reliance on frontal tactics cost a lot of lives. The advance moved southwards out of Assam and soon met with fierce Japanese resistance, but Wavell decided to maintain the offensive, at heavy cost. In April, General Slim took over from Wavell. He found the troops exhausted in spirit and in body, and decided to go over to the defensive. But he was unable to hold the Japanese and in May the British were pushed back over the border into Assam. Akyab Island, whose airfields had been the objective of this drive overland, remained in Japanese hands.

While the Arakan offensive was playing itself out, a ray of hope was generated by activities in the northern theatre, though this too was soon extinguished. In February 1942 Wavell had asked for Brigadier Orde Wingate to be sent to him. Wingate had carried out successful guerrilla operations in Ethiopia against the Italians, and Wavell believed that he could be of use in a similar form of activity in Burma. He wanted Wingate to set up and train Long Range Penetration Groups, which would be used to strike at enemy communications and outposts. They must be specially trained to match the Japanese soldier's skill in jungle fighting, and must take instruction in radio communications and demolition techniques. While on missions behind the enemy lines they would be supplied by air.

206

Burma

CHINA

Dimapur

Laung Chaung

Kohima

Myitkyina

Yunnan

Assam

Ukhrul

Tonzang

Mogaung

Homalin

Silchar

Imphal

Palel

Pinlebu

Tamu

Mawlaik

Tiddim

Kalewa

Thabeikkyin

Myinmu

Ye-U-

Lashio

Bishenpur

Monywa

Shwebo

**Eastern
Bengal**

Chittagong

Mandalay

Gangaw

Myingyan Pagan

Maymyo

Pauk

Meiktila

B U R M A

Buthidaung

Chauk

Thazi

Maungdaw

Pakokku

Pyawbwe

Seikpyu

Yamethin

Akyab Island

Yenanyaung

Myothit

Pyinmana

Toungoo

Prome

Penwegan

Pegu

Rangoon

Moulmein

Bay of Bengal

THAILAND

Arakan

Salween

Gulf of Siam

Imphal and Rangoon

◀▼
Chindits cross a river behind enemy lines
as they drive towards the Irrawaddy.

▼
Brigadier Orde Wingate at a briefing
during the Chindit operation behind the
Japanese lines in early 1943.

207

A hit scored on a Japanese train by RAF
aircraft in Burma.

In February 1943 the Chindits, as
this special force had been named,
crossed the Chindwin in two groups.
Moving eastwards, they struck at
bridges, railway lines and Japanese
outposts, and in mid-March crossed
the Irrawaddy. The Japanese by now
had despatched troops to deal with
this destructive nuisance, and the
Chindits, threatened by superior
Japanese forces, were forced to
withdraw, arriving back in India in
mid-April. The operation had yielded
little in the way of strategic gains,

but it had proved that the Japanese
were not the sole masters of the art
of jungle warfare. To the Japanese,
it demonstrated the inadequacy of
the Chindwin as a barrier, and this in
part contributed to their decision to
advance across it into India the
following year.

Allied leaders now considered
plans for the future. One of these
involved a seaborne invasion of
Rangoon, but this was shelved because there were no resources available for such an operation. The

Americans were anxious to re-establish overland communications with China via the Burma road from Mandalay, and therefore operations for the next dry season (November 1943–May 1944) were, it was finally decided, to be concentrated in north Burma.

In August, Lord Louis Mountbatten was appointed head of the newly formed South East Asia Command, with General Stilwell as his deputy, and Allied strength on land and in the air was built up in preparation for the offensive. The Japanese correctly interpreted the Allies' intention, and themselves began to lay plans for an advance across the border aimed at securing the logistically important Imphal plain and the mountain passes from Assam. If successful, this would put paid to Allied schemes for the reconquest of Burma.

The British central offensive was preceded, as planned, by a new Arakan offensive and a Chindit spearhead attack. In the Arakan theatre

▲▲
A Grant tank fords a river during the Imphal–Kohima battle.

▲
British troops after crossing the Chindwin in December 1944 during Operation Capital.

General Stilwell (front-seat passenger in the leading jeep), deputy head of South East Asia Command and commander of American and Chinese forces in Burma.

A P-40 Tomahawk of the 'Flying Tigers', originally a group of American volunteer pilots who defended the road to Burma and gave air support to the Chinese army. In July 1942 they were incorporated into the USAAF.

US troops cross a rubber pontoon bridge south of Myitkyina on the way to the Burma road.

◀ The first convoy for China moves off from Ledo, Assam, towards Kunming.

▼ British troops clearing out snipers from pagodas on Mandalay Hill after the capture of Mandalay.

Four-cannoned Spitfires on their way to the Burma battlefront.

A Japanese soldier shot dead in his foxhole. He holds an aerial bomb which he would have detonated, at the expense of his life, when a tank passed over.

14th Army tanks churn forward in the advance towards Rangoon.

▲
A member of a Sikh patrol throws a
phosphorous grenade to winkle out Japanese
defenders, lying in the path of the advance,
out of their foxholes.

▶▲
Paratroops were dropped at strategic
points round Rangoon on May 1, 1945, in
advance of the seaborne landings. The
picture shows a Japanese machine-gun and
its crew silenced by them.

◀
Landing craft go up-river towards
Rangoon, with smoke rising from the
bombed city.

▶▶
Members of the RAF Regiment
manhandling anti-aircraft guns through a
sea of mud on the Rangoon beachhead.

British troops began advancing southwards towards Akyab Island at the
beginning of 1944. In February the
Japanese launched their own offensive in Arakan and the British advance
was halted, then cut off by a Japanese
sweep westwards towards the coast.
Previous British tactical ideas would
have dictated a withdrawal at this
point, but Slim had evolved a new
system whereby the outflanked force
would retreat into a stronghold established during the advance and sit it
out, with air supply, until reinforcements moved up and tackled the
encircling enemy. In practice this
tactic was now seen to work, and
the Japanese abandoned their
offensive.

Meanwhile the Chindit operation
had got under way. Wingate had
top-level support from the Allied
leaders, and his force had been considerably increased in strength. Additionally, he had changed his ideas

about the function of his Long
Range Penetration Groups: in this
new mission he would discard his
earlier hit-and-run methods in favour
of establishing forward positions and,
with the benefit of airborne supplies,
holding on to them and making gains
from them. Thus his expedition
would be the spearhead of the subsequent thrust southwards from behind him. On March 5, 1944, the
Chindits set off, aiming for Indaw
and the surrounding area on the Irrawaddy, and were soon within striking
distance of their objective. Though
initially taken by surprise, the Japanese quickly sent reinforcements to
Indaw, and on March 26 the 16th
LRP Brigade's attack on Indaw was
beaten off. Wingate himself had been
killed in a plane crash two days
earlier, but even before his death the
operations of the various Chindit
groups had begun to get out of gear,
and in April the Chindits were moved

Battle of Imphal — Kohima

Kohima

Road to Dimapur

Imphal

Tamu

Tiddim

Kohima

Road to Dimapur

Imphal

Tamu

Tiddim

■ Japanese forces   □ British forces   ◯ Positions held   ▨ Positions lost

northwards to join Stilwell.

The Chindits' efforts behind the lines had failed to disrupt the Japanese offensive, which got under way in mid-March. It involved two main thrusts: one at Imphal and the other a deep, flanking move at Kohima. With some difficulty, owing to the fact that their forces were widely scattered at the time, the British were able to organise defensive positions on the Imphal plain, but they were not quick enough to strengthen the 1,500-strong garrison at Kohima, and to make matters worse the Japanese cut the road between Kohima and Imphal.

For a while the position appeared bleak, but on May 10, a week after the attack on Kohima, General Slim ordered a counter-offensive, and on May 18, after bitter fighting, the Kohima garrison was relieved and the surrounding Japanese driven off. There was a fierce struggle round Imphal, too, but the British soon had the upper hand, being superior in numbers of men and aircraft. The Japanese commander, General Mutaguchi, refused to allow his hard-pressed troops to withdraw, forcing them to maintain the offensive long after all hope of victory had gone. Consequently, Japanese losses came to over 50,000 in contrast with 17,000 on the British side.

Success in the Imphal-Kohima

◄
Pathans of a Punjab regiment move up on a Japanese position during mopping-up operations.

▲▲
Singapore, September 12, 1945. Admiral Mountbatten countersigns the document confirming the Japanese surrender in South East Asia.

▲
The Japanese surrender to the Allies in Rangoon.

episode indicated to the Allies that the Japanese hold on Burma was at last weakened – but it had not been broken. During the rainy season of 1944 the Allies planned for a final, central thrust southwards towards Mandalay and Rangoon. In October, Operation Capital was launched. Allied strength had been considerably increased, while the Japanese received no reinforcements, priority now being given to halting the Americans' progress in the South West Pacific. Coupled with the

central thrust came another advance into Arakan, this time successful and resulting in the capture of Akyab Island with its airbases. In the meantime Stilwell's Chinese forces were advancing southwards towards the flank of the Burma road via Myitkyina. The road was cleared in April 1945.

Slim had planned to drive southwards and encircle the retreating Japanese forces near Meiktila, and though the Japanese fought to break out, the plan worked. The way to Rangoon therefore lay open, and General Messervy's force moved rapidly towards it, mopping up Japanese remnants on the way.

On May 1 Operation Dracula, the seaborne assault on Rangoon, was launched. The Japanese were already evacuating the city, and the Allied forces were soon in possession. On May 6 they met up with Messervy north of Rangoon. The Japanese occupation of Burma was at an end, and there only remained the task of clearing Japanese remnants from the country.

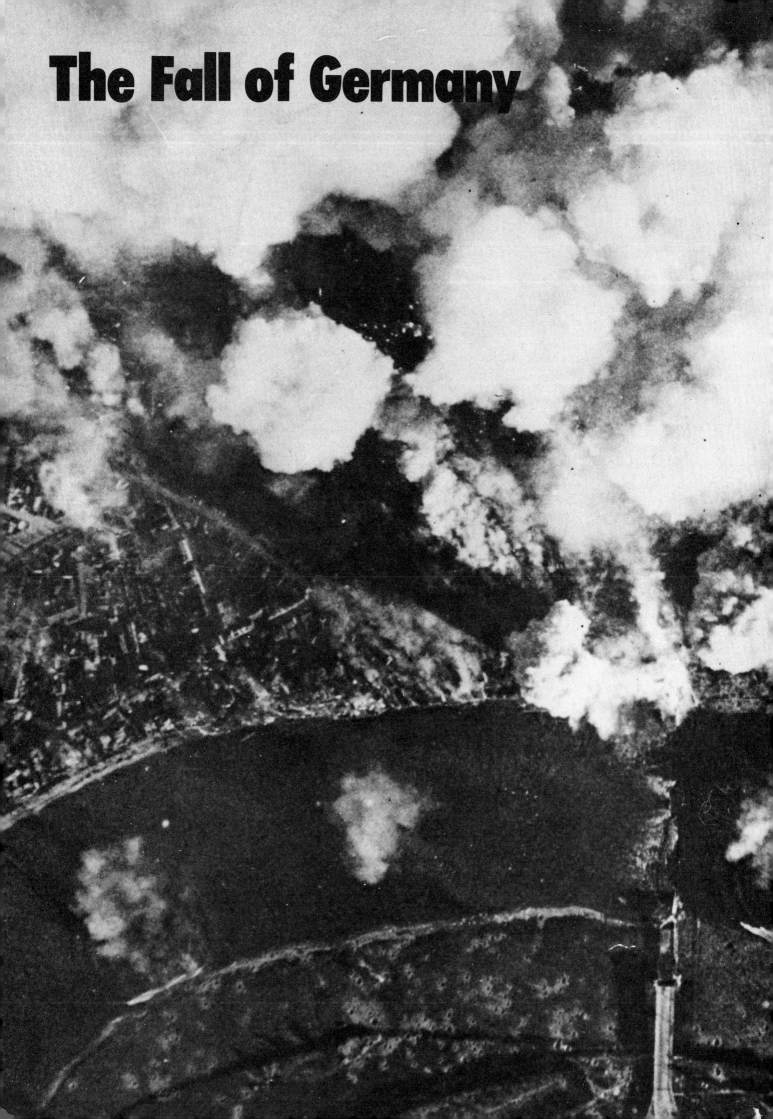

The Fall of Germany

An Allied bomber over Cologne during a daylight raid in October 1944.

Towards the end of 1944 the Allied advance on Germany had slowed down. In spite of a major offensive in mid-November, they were still thirty miles away from the vital sector of the Rhine that covered the Ruhr, the heart of Germany's war-industrial effort. Allied bombing by night and day was making the maintenance of necessary production levels harder and harder to achieve, but Hitler's war machine could not be halted until the factories of the Ruhr were put out of action.

In the Allied armies there was a mood of ebullient optimism. France and Belgium had been liberated with surprising ease. It was only a matter of keeping up the pressure until the German line broke.

The Allied strategic bombing offensive continued till the end of the war, industrial targets being hit with ever greater success after the Normandy invasion. German cities had been bombed from early on, often with terrible effect. One such city was Cologne, pictured here, of which 600 acres were devastated after a 1,000-bomber raid in May 1942.

Albert Speer, Hitler's production chief, who fought a losing battle to keep the wheels of the war machine turning.

US soldiers carry off a wounded comrade in a war-torn German town.

▲
American troops file up to the front during the Battle of the Bulge.
◀
On the northern flank of the Bulge, an Allied tank passes another being dug out.
▶
A US transport drops supplies to American troops cut off in Bastogne during the Battle of the Bulge.

226

There was some consternation, therefore, when German forces made a breakthrough in the Ardennes on December 16. What was going on? Was this a defiant gesture or a major offensive? By the time the Allies stopped them, the Germans had carved a hole sixty-five miles deep in Allied-held territory.

Hitler had been planning a counter-offensive for some months past. He had scraped together and re-equipped his last reserves of strength in men and armour for a scheme which was entirely his own idea, and which he had planned down to the last detail. Even the generals whom he chose to execute his last orders could make only slight modifications to them, and then only after protracted reasoning with him. The plan was inspired, if over-ambitious. Manteuffel and Dietrich would break through in the Ardennes with two panzer armies and, driving northwards via Antwerp and Brussels, would cut off the Allied armies and precipitate a second Dunkirk. He banked on poor weather restricting the Allied air forces' operations against his advancing armies.

◄

The execution of Germans arrested wearing American uniforms behind Allied lines. Hitler sent a party of them in advance of his Ardennes counter-offensive to disrupt Allied communications.

◄ ▼

Against the backcloth of the ruins of Cologne Cathedral, an American tank sustains a direct hit from a German tank (not in picture). One of the tank's crew struggles to get out. The Americans entered Cologne in March 1945, just before the Rhine crossings.

►

Hitler discusses the situation on the Oder–Neisse line with his generals in March 1945. It was to reinforce his eastern defences that he stripped his western front after the failure of the Ardennes counter-offensive.

▼

The Rhine bridge at Remagen, captured intact by US troops on March 7, 1945. The first, though limited, Rhine crossing was made here.

◄◄ Allied aircraft fly low over the Rhine as supplies are ferried across.

◄ This rubber pontoon bridge across the Rhine was built in the record time of six and a half hours.

◄▼ Just after the Rhine crossings in the West, Red Army troops took the port of Danzig from the Germans in the East. The picture shows Russian infantry in the centre of the town.

► An American bomber breaking up in the sky over Germany, April 1945. It was one of the 22,948 USAAF aircraft lost in combat operations.

▼ RAF Lancasters on a daylight bombing raid, 1943. The Lancaster could be adapted to carry a single bomb of up to 22,000 lb, the heaviest carried by any aircraft during the war.

In spite of unpleasant memories of the Germans' surprise breakthrough in the Ardennes in 1940, which had come with catastrophic swiftness, the Allied line in this sector was weak, only four divisions covering an eighty-mile stretch. German troop movements in the sector had been reported, but these failed to provoke an Allied reaction. When the breakthrough came, its initial impact and its early progress were considerable.

Hitler prepared the way for his armies by sending through the Allied lines a handful of commando infiltrators, wearing American uniforms and travelling in American vehicles, who created confusion by such disruptive tactics as cutting telephone wires and pointing signposts in the wrong direction. When some of these commandos were captured, even more confusion was created, for how could an American-clad German be distinguished from an American? Nobody escaped a grilling.

The initial penetrations made by the offensive brought the Germans to Bastogne, a vital road centre, on December 19. The American defenders held them off, however, and after a few days Manteuffel was forced to by-pass the town, which held out until the advance had halted.

But the drive westwards was slowing down. The Allies were piling on more pressure every hour, mud was bogging down the vehicles, and the old bogy of fuel shortage reared its head. By December 26 the advance had been stopped. There had been heavy losses on both sides, and the Americans had had their fiercest fight since the Normandy landings, while the bulge created by the German spearheads was over sixty miles deep and forty-five miles wide. At their furthest point of advance, they were

◄▲
American soldiers search for snipers in the wreckage of the bombed-out Krupp steel plant in Essen, captured on April 10, 1945.

◄
Russian tanks grind through the shattered streets of Berlin, where they met desperate German resistance. The Red Army entered Berlin in the third week of April.

◄▼
Ten days before his suicide, a weary Hitler stares bleakly into the camera on his last birthday.

►
American, British and Russian troops in the ruins of Hitler's Chancellery.

▼
The historic meeting of Russian and Allied forces on the Elbe at the end of April 1945. Marshal Rokossovsky shakes hands with Montgomery.

Some of the prisoners taken by the Russians in Berlin.

Hungry German civilians looting a freight train in Frankfurt in search of food and clothing.

The captured Focke-Wulf aircraft factory in Bremen, bombed by the RAF.

Montgomery reads the surrender terms to the Germans on May 4 in his temporary HQ on Lüneburg Heath.

Saved in the nick of time. A former inmate of Belsen concentration camp, too weak to dress, is helped into clean clothes. Allied liberating forces opened the eyes of the world to the indescribable horror of what they saw in camps such as this.

only four miles short of the Meuse at Dinant.

Although the Allies now plainly had the advantage, Hitler refused to countenance a withdrawal. On the contrary, he threw in fresh troops, squandering his meagre reserves, only to find these beaten back day by day at heavy cost. Then, in January, as pressure on his eastern front threatened, he withdrew all available forces to throw them against the Russians. The counter-offensive had gained only a few weeks' respite, and had cost Hitler a large part of his remaining strength.

Now the Allies thrust forward. On March 7 Patton's 3rd Army reached the Rhine at Coblenz. Further north, the 1st Army boldly took the bridge at Remagen, near Bonn, which was still substantially intact, and here a limited crossing took place. On March 22 Patton crossed the Rhine at Oppenheim, and on March 23 Montgomery's gigantic assault be-

gan, on the Rhine near Wesel. The last barrier was down, and on April 11, 1945, the Allied armies reached the Elbe, only sixty miles west of Berlin.

Resuming his offensive on the Oder on April 16, Zhukov thrust his armies through the German defences, and a week later the Russians were fighting the last, desperate remnants of Hitler's armies in the streets of Berlin. By April 25 Berlin was surrounded, and two days later the Russians met the Allies on the Elbe.

The formalities of surrender remained. Hitler poisoned himself on April 30 in his Berlin bunker, and it was left to his generals to conclude arrangements. On May 2 German forces in Italy surrendered, and on May 4 Admiral Dönitz signed a surrender document at Montgomery's HQ on Lüneburg Heath. Later, he and his colleagues would stand trial at Nuremberg, the expression of the world's bitter condemnation of the Third Reich.

235

The Fall of Japan

US landing-craft head for the beaches of Luzon in January 1945 under cover of a naval bombardment. The capture of the island more or less completed MacArthur's reconquest of the Philippines.

A Japanese aircraft dives blazing into the sea astern of a US carrier off Saipan in the Marianas.

US Sherman tanks assemble for a mopping-up patrol near Hollandia, New Guinea, in May 1944.

April and May 1944 saw Allied landings near Hollandia, on the north coast of Dutch New Guinea, on the offshore island of Wakde, and on Biak Island, beyond Wakde. With these positions secured, it was time to prepare for the next stage, the conquest of the Marianas. There were Japanese garrisons on Saipan, Tinian and Guam, the group representing an important staging-post in Japan's communications with her South West Pacific empire. For the Americans, bases on the islands would put their B-29 Superfortresses within easy bombing range of Japan and the Philippines.

An invasion armada was assembled, with 130,000 troops on board, and on June 15 the US Marines landed on Saipan. The Japanese had planned an operation to counter the American invasion. The aim of this was to crush the American fleet between a carrier force advancing eastwards towards the islands and land-based aircraft flying westwards from the island, and as the landings got under way Admiral Toyoda's fleet steamed into the Philippine sea in the opening stages of the plan. On June 19 the Battle of the Philippine Sea took place, the Japanese facing Admiral Spruance's enormously powerful 5th Fleet. The Japanese position was weakened by their inability to apply pressure on the Americans with land-based aircraft, as the Japanese air forces on the Marianas had already largely been wiped out, and they suffered a resounding defeat. In the two phases of the battle they lost nearly 500 aircraft and three fleet carriers, while many of their other ships were damaged. Their withdrawal removed any real possibility of obstruction of subsequent American progress to

239

◀ ▲

Admiral William F. Halsey, commander of
the US 3rd Fleet, which wiped out a
Japanese carrier force off the Philippines
during the Battle of Leyte Gulf.

◀

American troops began landing on Leyte
Island, in the middle of the Philippines, in
October. The picture shows General
MacArthur, commander-in-chief in the
South West Pacific, going ashore.

US Marines stand with rifles ready in case any Japanese troops escape the effects of demolition charges hurled into a gun nest on Saipan. After the Japanese defeat in the Battle of the Philippine Sea, the conquest of the Marianas went ahead unhindered. The islands offered airfields within range of Japan and the Philippines.

the Philippines, and allowed the invasion of the Marianas to proceed unhindered. Landings took place on Guam on July 21, and on Tinian on July 23, and though Japanese resistance was stubborn and fierce, the conquest of the islands was never in doubt.

The next target was the Philippines Islands, whose defence was led by General Yamashita, commander of the victorious Japanese forces in Malaya in 1942. After the capture of Morotai Island (south of Mindanao) and the Palau Islands in September, MacArthur's forces landed at Leyte on October 20. This island lay in the middle of the Philippine chain; possession of it would divide the Japanese defence in two. The Japanese were determined to hold the Philippines, and had planned a baited trap for the

American invasion fleet. The bait was to be a naval force, including four carriers, under Admiral Ozawa, which was to sail south from Japan in the hope of decoying the US fleet into coming to meet it. This would lay open to attack the invasion transports and their escorts off Leyte. To crush them Admiral Kurita would sail up from Singapore, dividing his force to attack from the north-west and the south-west in a pincer movement. For this operation he relied entirely on traditional warships, including the massive 18-inch-gun battleships *Yamato* and *Musashi*.

This appeared a sound enough scheme on paper, but in practice it demanded that the Americans do everything they were expected to do. Moreover the decision to use big guns as the main striking force, when carriers had proved their supremacy

◄◄
Pilots and crewmen of the aircraft carrier
Enterprise get ready to launch a
reconnaissance patrol of Grumman Hellcat
fighter-bombers during the Battle of
Leyte Gulf.

►
US troops on Corregidor cleaning out a
suicide squad of Japanese in a shell hole;
many would have grenades strapped to
their waists. Few surrendered.

▲▲
The Japanese battleship-carrier *Ise*. She
carried four 14-inch guns forward and a
launching deck aft.

▲
US troops building sandbag piers out to
LSTs off Leyte to facilitate unloading.

US Marines head for the beaches of Iwo Jima, where 2,500 of them were lost on the first day.

Marines dash across the black volcanic sand on an Iwo Jima beach, dragging equipment.

Rocket launchers in action in Iwo Jima.

in this role, was a mistake. In any event, things went wrong for the Japanese from the start. Kurita's fleet was spotted in time for the US admirals to make preparations, and their preoccupation with his approach resulted in failure to notice the approach of Ozawa's decoy force — in spite of his desperate attempts, by sending out uncoded signals, to attract attention. Before long Halsey's carrier planes were attacking Kurita's fleet in waves, sinking the *Musashi* and forcing the Japanese to steam away. Halsey took this as signifying a final withdrawal, and, having at last learned of Ozawa's approach, he raced off northwards with his entire fleet to meet him. No sooner had he done so than he received a reconnaissance report stating that Kurita had turned round and was heading back into battle. Now set on destroying Ozawa's fleet, he was disinclined to believe the report and steamed on northwards. He was convinced that, even if it were true, the Japanese fleet had been so reduced by the first encounter that Admiral Kinkaid's fleet would easily be able to repulse the second onslaught without his help. Kinkaid, for his part, was not aware that Halsey had left no ships guarding

the northern approach, via the San Bernadino Strait, and was content to watch the southern approach, the Surigao Strait. When Kurita's southern force arrived, it was forced to steam in line ahead through the narrow strait, and in a classic crossing of the 'T', the Americans blew the Japanese ships out of the water.

The victory was complete when news arrived of the Japanese northern fleet, which had already started attacking the small force guarding MacArthur's invasion vessels. Kinkaid signalled to Halsey to return, but Halsey steamed on. Now the Japanese, having cleared the opposition out of the way, moved in on the defenceless transports. Kinkaid signalled to Halsey again, and at last Halsey turned back — but he had gone so far that his arrival was hours away.

At this point Kurita suddenly turned away. Intercepted radio messages had convinced him that the Americans were about to cut off his escape route, and he raced off to tackle this phantom threat.

The Battle of Leyte Gulf was, miraculously, over. It had been the largest naval engagement of all time in terms of numbers of ships involved. Though the Japanese battleships

The US fleet carrier *Franklin* burning and listing to starboard after being attacked by Kamikaze aircraft in March 1945.

Kamikaze pilots have their group photograph taken before going out to die. They carry their samurai swords, the mark of the warrior.

The giant 18-inch-gun Japanese battleship *Yamato* trying to dodge bombs from US carrier-based aircraft as she heads for Okinawa. This amounted to a Kamikaze mission, for she had no fuel for a return journey and no air cover. After two hours, during which she received bomb and torpedo hits, she sank. This was proof, if any more were needed, that the day of the battleship was over.

escaped, their aircraft carriers (in Ozawa's force) had all four been sunk, and their lack of carriers now spelt the end of Japanese seapower. They had, however, demonstrated for the first time a new, almost un-stoppable weapon, the Kamikaze suicide aircraft, which was to claim many victims.

By Christmas 1944 Japanese resistance on Leyte Island was at an end, and on January 3, 1945, an American fleet of 164 ships set sail from Leyte Gulf to effect landings on the main Philippine island of Luzon. On January 8 the landings took place in Lingayen Gulf, north of Manila, and soon American forces were pushing southwards towards

the capital. By March 4, after hand-to-hand fighting in the streets, Manila was in American hands, while the Bataan peninsula and the island of Corregidor (both scenes of earlier American defeats) had been captured.

Two stepping-stones now lay between the Americans and Japan: the islands of Iwo Jima and Okinawa. Iwo Jima, offering bomber bases only half as far from Tokyo as the Marianas bases, was tackled first. This four-mile-long island was held by a 25,000-strong Japanese garrison, which had dug itself well in. Admiral Spruance, commander of the operation, unleashed a heavy aerial and naval bombardment before

▲▲
An American flame-throwing tank pours fire at a Japanese position on an Okinawa hillside.

▲
A scene on an Okinawa landing beach. Landings began on April 1, 1945.

tified. Okinawa, almost equidistant from Formosa, Japan and China, was a desirable strategic objective, but the Americans realised they would need to employ an enormous force to take it. Airfields in Japan were attacked in advance of the invasion to minimise the threat from Japanese air forces, and over a quarter of a million troops were assembled.

On April 1 landings took place on the west coast towards the south of the island. Surprisingly, Japanese interference was minimal, and a beachhead was easily established. By April 3 the island had been crossed, but a move southwards provoked stiffer opposition. Hundreds of Kamikaze aircraft assailed the invaders—even the battleship *Yamato*, on April 6, was sent on a pointless suicide mission, without fuel for a return voyage, culminating in her loss with appalling casualties.

American forces now pressed northward and southward. On April 19 a major attack was launched on Japanese positions in the south, but they were well dug-in and the attackers suffered considerable casualties for little gain.

Now the Japanese were becoming impatient. After adhering strictly to the ordained policy of stubborn defence, they launched a counter-offensive at the beginning of May. This achieved a penetration, but the assault was beaten off with Japanese losses of 5,000. By early June they had been forced down into the

putting the Marines ashore on February 19, but even so the Americans suffered 2,500 casualties on that day. After a savage struggle, resistance ceased on March 26. American losses amounted to 26,000, but the Japanese garrison literally fought to the death, only a few hundred being taken prisoner.

On Okinawa, the Japanese had built up their strength to 110,000. This was a much larger island, with rugged terrain, and once again the Japanese positions were deeply for-

extreme south of the island, and in the middle of the month, after extensive employment of flame-throwers, a breakthrough was achieved. In this battle the Japanese had employed massed Kamikaze raids and had fought with terrible deter-mination, but, significantly, a much larger proportion gave themselves up at the end. Their losses were 110,000 against the Americans' 45,000.

While mopping-up operations proceeded in various quarters, Japan

Hiroshima after the atom bomb, which was dropped on August 6, 1945.

was subjected to a massive stepping-up of American bombing raids, which had started in October 1944 from the Marianas. Though cut off from essential supplies, and with her war production decimated, she refused to capitulate on the Allies' unconditional terms. Finally, a resort was made to the new atomic bombs: one was dropped on Hiroshima on August 6, another on Nagasaki on August 9. On September 2, aboard the US battleship *Missouri*, the Japanese surrendered.